# BION'S DREAM

# BION'S DREAM

## A reading of the autobiographies

*Meg Harris Williams*

Routledge
Taylor & Francis Group

LONDON AND NEW YORK

Published 2010 by Karnac Books Ltd

Published 2018 by Routledge
2 Park Square, Milton Park, Abingdon, Oxon OX14 4RN
711 Third Avenue, New York, NY 10017, USA

*Routledge is an imprint of the Taylor & Francis Group, an informa business*

British Library Cataloguing in Publication Data

A C.I.P. for this book is available from the British Library

ISBN 978 1 85575 890 2 (pbk)


Edited, designed, and produced by The Studio Publishing Services Ltd
www.publishingservicesuk.co.uk
e-mail: studio@publishingservicesuk.co.uk

# CONTENTS

*ACKNOWLEDGEMENTS*

I would like to thank the editors of the following journals in which parts of this book were first published: *International Review of Psycho-analysis,* "'Underlying Pattern' in Bion's *Memoir of the Future"*, Vol. 10 (75), 1983, pp. 75–86; *Journal of Child Psychotherapy,* "Bion's *The Long Week-End*: a review article", Vol. 9, 1983, pp. 69–79; and *Free Associations,* "The Tiger and 'O'", Vol. 1, 1985, pp. 33–55.

*To Francesca Bion*

Meg Harris Williams is a writer and visual artist with a lifelong psychoanalytic education; her mother was Martha Harris of the Tavistock Clinic, and her stepfather Donald Meltzer. She read English at Cambridge and Oxford universities and her first book to marry poetic and psychoanalytic epistemologies was *Inspiration in Milton and Keats* (1981). Since then she has continued to write on the poetic origins of psychoanalytic thinking and the aesthetic implications for psychoanalysis in many books and articles including *A Strange Way of Killing* (1987), *The Apprehension of Beauty* (1988, with Donald Meltzer), *The Chamber of Maiden Thought* (1992, with Margot Waddell), *A Trial of Faith: Horatio's Story* (1996), *The Vale of Soulmaking: the post-Kleinian model of the mind and its poetic origins* (2005) and *The Aesthetic Development: the poetic spirit of psychoanalysis* (2010). She has also written and illustrated a book of Shakespeare stories for children, *Five Tales from Shakespeare* (1996). She is editor of the Harris Meltzer Trust publications. Websites: www.artlit.info and www.harris-meltzer-trust.org.uk

I am: therefore I question. It is the answer—the "yes, I know"—that is the disease which kills ... The song the sirens sing, and always have sung, is that the arrival at the inn—not the journey—is the reward, the prize, the heaven, the cure.

[Wilfred Bion, *All My Sins Remembered*]

I know nothing. I ask.
When one replies to me,
I mark what is said
In bone and artery.
Blood says: this is true,
And that's but a mask.

[Roland Harris, "I ask a fresh vision"]

# Introduction

From the time of *Transformations* (1965), Bion began to integrate his earlier work on groups with his quest to understand the individual psyche, and it became increasingly clear that this is an aesthetic quest. The individual is himself a "group of thoughts and feelings" and the method of psychoanalysis is to discern and describe their "underlying pattern": "I wonder what I do when trying to draw an analysand's attention to a pattern" (Bion, 1991, p. 213). In the realm of aesthetic patterns, "Psychoanalysis is just a stripe on the coat of the tiger. Ultimately it may meet the Tiger—the Thing Itself—O" (*ibid.*, p. 112). The "ferocious animal Absolute Truth" may not be capturable, but the "great hunters" of psychoanalytic intuition can interpret from shadowy glimpses, provided they are free to have nightmares rather than being confined to "the pale illumination of daylight" (pp. 5, 239).

Bion's autobiographical narratives *A Memoir of the Future* (1975–1979)[1] and *The Long Week-End* (1982), together with its sequel *All My Sins Remembered* (1985), are the key to his self-analysis of internal groupings and their shifting patterns. These books, therefore, represent the most finely honed examples of his teaching method. The "model of actual physical warfare" may be used as a storyline, but the real subject is always the "war of the mind", and "from that warfare there is no release"—a phrase from "before psychoanalysis was even thought of" (Bion, 2005a, p. 93). At the end of his life, he strove to present not just his life-story, and not just his thoughts, but his mode of thinking, in terms of an internal conversation which might be sufficiently realistic in its form as to become "audible to others" (1991, p. 113). His ambition is none other than to dramatize the process of thinking itself: the type of thinking which, however imperfectly, "shapes the thinker", and whose reality is seen rather in the changing shape of a mind than in any theory, message, or summary of experience.

Looking back over his own romance with psychoanalysis, Bion tells us that instead of "feeling-it-in-the-past" as with his first analyst, he realized he needed to know how to deal with his feelings of the present; this meant getting back in touch with his native "spark of sincerity" (Bion, 1985, p. 45). He compares his mind to a smouldering fire awaiting reignition:

> Don't interrupt [Bion says to himself]; I'm thinking. It would be useful if I could search through the debris of my mind, the ashy remnants of what once was a flaming fire, in the hope of revealing some treasure which would reconstitute a valuable piece of wisdom—a spark amidst the ashes that could be blown into a flame at which others could warm their hands. [*ibid.*, p. 31]

He offers his own mind as a potential fount of vitality at which others might "warm their hands" if they, too, can seek out the generative spark of sincerity, coextensive—he says—with the "sleeping beauty" of psychoanalysis itself.

*The Long Week-End* has joined the classic narratives of the First World War and is easy to read and empathize with; but the *Memoir* is probably still, as Francesca Bion has said, the least understood of Bion's works. As my mother, Martha Harris,[2] has written:

> [Bion's] own intuitive thinking was so far in advance of anyone else's in our field that its seminal effect can only begin to be felt. Such is the impact of *A Memoir of the Future*, which traces the complex mind in action, talking from many vertices, from the whole gamut of his years—the foetus in the womb to the 77-year-

old . . . it presents the living drama of his internal history; amusing, argumentative, profound, puzzling, always unexpected, sometimes blindingly, obviously true. [1980; Harris, 1987a, p. 344]

The *Memoir*, described as a "fictitious account of psychoanalysis" (Bion, 1991, p. 4) is clearly and explicitly an artificial dream, searching for aesthetic form in a genre of its own. It is Em-mature's "psycho-embryonic attempt to write an embryo-scientific account of a journey from birth to death" (p. 429). The story covers an entire lifetime and yet, in another sense—like William Golding's dream of a drowning man, *Pincher Martin*—could be taken as dreamed in an instant. As T. S. Eliot put it:

> We had the experience but missed the meaning,
> And approach to the meaning restores the experience
> In a different form, beyond any meaning
> We can assign to happiness. ["The Dry Salvages", ll. 93–96]

The meaning lies in the process as aesthetic object—the "living drama of an internal history"—not the accidents of life, but their usage as a metaphorical representation of mental life. It is the dreamed meaning that has a "seminal effect" and that ignites sparks in other people and engages their own self-analytic "restorative experience".

Something of this "dreamed" quality inheres also in the more literal autobiographies, by contrast with Bion's war diaries, for example. These, too, are essentially internal narratives: as Bion says, "I write about 'me'" (1982, p. 8). In this lies their universal and psychological (as distinct from historical) interest. In a piece of dialogue between internal voices in *Sins*, Bion says:

> I think you've got it muddled up.
> *I don't mind if I have because I'm not telling the story of my life. Those who want to write the story of their lives have a problem: that problem is not mine.* [1985, p. 33]

The statement (from one part of himself) that he is *not* telling the story of his life may appear obscure, until we recognize that his main concern in writing the narrative is to do with living his life in the present; as he explains elsewhere:

> The reason why we concern ourselves with things that are remem-
> bered, with our past history, is not because of what it was—
> although that might be quite important in its own right—but
> because of the mark it has left on you or me or us *now*. [Bion, 1997,
> p. 38]

Paradoxically as it may seem, it is this "mark *now*" that will give
the story a chance to endure. What he is really remembering is the
pattern of his mental development, a continuing evolution that
involves making contact with the internal child from the time when
he was not a "bloody fool" (as he often felt himself to be, after going
on permanent "home leave" from his "poor little ignorant Indian
self"): " I think I remember, or imagine—I don't even now know
which—that there was a time when I was not [a bloody fool]" (1985,
p. 32).[3] When he was the "Elephant's Child" of "insatiable curiosity" he was a different, more Shakespearean, kind of fool with an
appetite for learning;[4] and rediscovering this internal aspect is what
provides the vital spark for each new story or spiritual journey that
he undertakes.

At the very foundation of the perennial dream-story lies the
phantasized mating between Bion's internal parents. His father,
Bion tells us, "hunted with Jim Corbett" and thereby acquires (in
internal reality) something of his environmental intuition and heroism—the man who, as we learn from *Man-Eaters of Kumaon* (1944),[5]
lived on the caesura between the tiger-mind and the human one,
sensitive to the emotional upheavals of this delicate borderland
between jungle and habitation. Complementing the hunter–father
in this mental landscape is the mysterious female, tigerish spirit
embodied in his ayah and part-Indian mother with her lush "abandoned" hats. Here lies the hidden richness that enabled him to
"stick close to the fighting line" and to mentally survive the various
traumas of his life.

When Bion speculates in the *Memoir* on the blush on the walls
of the uterus that occurs with the mating of sperm and ovum (1991,
p. 566), and that occurs each time a new idea is conceived, he is
re-dreaming the origins of his own mind—newly infused with
meaning once again, casting off the coverings of respectability.
For "This is an attempt to express my rebellion—to say "Goodbye"
to all that" (p. 578). Goodbye to the "cant" of his "overpowering"
non-conformist upbringing, to the cant of kosher Kleinianism, to

the confines of all types of respectable "hero dress" that imprison the "growing germ of thought". At the end of his life, therefore, Bion was committed to following his own advice to "abandon himself" to the Platonic Idea of psychoanalysis, incarnate in the form of his self-analysis. Yet what he said of the writers he admired applies also to his own autobiographies:

> How difficult it is to realise that with certain books one does not "read" them - one has to have an emotional experience of reading them. This seems so slow compared with the easy slick reading . . . [1985, p. 178]

It is no use going straight to the end of the book (i.e., the interpretation), as Bion satirises in his little dialogues between author and reader at the beginning and end of each volume of the *Memoir*. In an emotional experience of reading, we have to forego memory and desire and instead acquire a symbolic congruence with the writer's own story, to take it in and incorporate it in our own self-analysis.

This little book started life as a single chapter of *The Aesthetic Development* (Williams, 2010), on a basis of reprinting previous essays, but it outgrew its allotted shell. It concludes with a discussion of some of Bion's poetic "ancestors" (as he called them), an expanded version of an essay which Luiz Carlos Junqueira of the Brazilian Psychoanalytic Society asked me to write for publication in Portuguese (Williams, 2009). The influence of the poets on the deep grammar of Bion's theories has been little studied, so it seemed useful to give this implicit feature of his "autobiography" a chapter of its own, even though it is far from comprehensive. It enables us to step back a psychic generation in terms of the life of the spark of sincerity, to observe how the poets got into Bion in the same way that Bion (as well as the poets) can get into us. It demonstrates how thoughts are "generative", as the post-natal Group affirm in the *Memoir*.

Above all, in this book I have tried to avoid the "dependency" trap of which Martha Harris warned while Bion was still alive:

> The dependent group structure so often manifests itself in the reliance upon a crystallized selection of the theories of Freud (the original Messiah), sometimes pitted against a similar extrapolation from Melanie Klein (a latter day saint). Bion is unlikely to escape

the same fate. Their theories in such a climate of polarization are suitably selected and presented to eliminate the essential questioning, contradictions and progressions inherent in the formulations of pioneers who are constantly struggling to conceptualize the clinical observations they are making. [1978; Harris, 1987b, p. 328]

The delusion of possessing one's subject—so being in a position to judge and evaluate—is easily maintained when it has cultural or academic respectability. I do not wish to participate in a new orthodoxy; instead, here I have continued a personal search, begun thirty years ago, for living pieces of wisdom ever ready to be fanned into a flame. I want to write about Bion in a way that could only be written by myself, though I hope the picture may overlap with that of other readers. If we take what Bion says seriously, this is the way he would himself wish to be "remembered". Such is the goal of all serious writing, including literary criticism; as Bion constantly reminds us, there are no new ideas—it is only their rediscovery and digestion that is new. Thoughts can exist quite happily without a thinker; it is only the thinker who is modified.

## Notes

1. The *Memoir* was originally published in three separate volumes (*The Dream*, 1975; *The Past Presented*, 1977; *The Dawn of Oblivion*, 1979); followed by *A Key* (1981). References here are to the complete single-volume edition (Karnac, 1991).
2. Martha Harris had been a supervisee of Bion's.
3. In the *Memoir*, Bion writes that whether the instruction to adopt an exoskeleton took the form of "couvre-toi de gloire" or "couvre-toi de flanelle", he "felt a fool either way" (p. 442).
4. In childhood, Wilfred was compared to Kipling's "Elephant's Child", and in *Sins* he writes of "Me, the Elephant's Child, one who does not learn for all its questions" (1985, p. 51).
5. I remember being profoundly impressed by this book as a teenager, so when I encountered Bion's autobiography, the positive and mysterious associations outweighed the more deadening veneer of the Edwardian Arfer–Raj type of masculinity that, to some extent, held his father in its straitjacket.

# CHAPTER ONE

# Remembering*

## The Long Week-End

Wilfred Bion's *The Long Week-End* is a fascinating account of one man's failure to become an individual, to achieve integrity, to make emotional contact with his internal objects. It is remarkable in that it is a well-written, witty, artistic evocation of an apparently unprepossessing subject. It works on the lines of the questions posed in his *Memoir of the Future:* "Has anyone seen an artist paint a picture 'about' or 'of' something ugly which was nevertheless beautiful?" (Bion, 1991, p. 128). The genre of the work might be described as a hybrid drawn from *Goodbye to All That, Lord of the Flies,* and *1984.* For although its effect depends on the realistic description of a particular social climate, it has a futuristic quality which makes an essential contribution to its emotional impact. In the religion, prudery, and patriotism of the late Victorian age, one glimpses Big Brother in the form of a series of "false

---

*This chapter reprints a review article of *The Long Week-End* from the time of its original publication (Williams, 1983b),[1] followed by a reading of the subsequent continuation of Bion's autobiography in *All My Sins Remembered.*

parents", of perverse ideals of masculinity and femininity and education. These, despite the good and even loving intentions of several of the main characters, succeed in divorcing the child Wilfred from any genuine emotional contact with his parents (literal and metaphorical), or with his cultural heritage. "The parents, staff, all were caught in a web of undirected menace" for "Who could recognise danger in piety, ardent patriotism to school and games heroes?" (Bion, 1982, pp. 47, 92). As a child, Wilfred has yet to learn that the prep-school bully, Morgan, is not unique but an archetype; and "there were plenty more where that one came from, the source of the Morgans of this life" (*ibid.*, pp. 47–50). And Bion occasionally slips in, in parentheses, other remarks to remind us that the sinister "web" of that period continues in modern forms. But the main key to the present and future relevance of the book lies in our seeing it as an account of the failure of growth of an Everyman. As Bion brings to notice in his Preface, "Anyone can 'know' which school, regiment, colleagues, friends I write about. In all but the most superficial sense they would be wrong. I write about 'me'". For, in writing about "me", he recognizes that he is "more likely to approximate to [his] ambition" of formulating "phenomena as close as possible to noumena" (p. 8).

The book, then, describes the series of misunderstandings and humiliations which transform him rapidly into an "accomplished liar" who can slip neatly into the basic assumptions of a given code of behaviour: a process which enables him to feel less of an "outcaste"—that is, less of an individual. He describes this as the formation of an "exo-skeleton" under the eye of a terrifying, vengeful God, "Arf Arfer". This method of anti-education prevents him from learning anything from experience, even the experience of war, from which "I learnt nothing—presumably because at 19 I had become too set in my ways" (p. 193). For the setting of the mental sheath cannot serve the mind's expansion:

> neither the discipline of repetitive command, nor the "heaven" of middle class England, nor an exo-skeleton taking the place of a skeleton for an endo-skeletonous animal, can serve; still less in the domain of the mind. [p. 194]

After an anti-climactic year as best pupil and games captain, Wilfred leaves school preparing to "meet my father and mother", as if for the first time (for they virtually disappear during the school narrative). Instead of a true "meeting", however, he discovers that his internal self seems to have disappeared; his mother kisses "a chitinous semblance of a boy from whom a person had escaped. But I was imprisoned, unable to break out of the shell which adhered to me". The metaphor of the fledgeling who is unable to hatch out properly runs throughout the book. In the *Memoir*, it achieves a kind of completion when the officer "hatches" from his exo-skeletonous tank, as he finally achieves, almost involuntarily, a capacity for thought. "Obsessed by the fear of cowardice", the young man newly emerged from school looks around for various kinds of cover ("Couvre-toi de gloire" or "couvre-toi de flannelle"?) and, initially rejected for the Army, finds he has "no base on which to stand". Time and again, the memory of meeting with his mother threatens to undermine the basic assumption group of the moment; but it is only a threat, for she is implicated in the network of deceit, having double standards of love and social acceptability. The conflict for Wilfred is intolerable; he feels, on leaving the Training Camp, that

> I was cut off from my base. And the enemy was in full occupation of my mother. "Tomorrow to fresh woods and pastures new". [*Lycidas*]. Yes, *woods* you fool! It is there alone in the jungle that you have to live. [p. 114]

There is "no anaesthetic for those suffering home leave" (p. 115). The pain of the other kind of "warfare"—the "jungle" of lonely internal struggle, the "woods" of *Lycidas*—is not bearable precisely owing to the double standards, which suggest a kind of unintentional treachery within the Mother. There is no support, no catharsis for the night-time fears related to the "jungle" of his childhood in India and his "poor little ignorant Indian self" (p. 92), which becomes somehow symbolic of the squashed outcaste potential of emotional contact. As at school, daytime conformity leads to night-time fears: "I say Richards, you *were* making a row last night! . . . as if you were being strangled!" (p. 90).

Bion makes clear that the "war" itself is simply the continuation of a pre-existing state of affairs, *ad absurdum*: "schoolboys of all ages playing soldiers, rehearsing for the real thing, but never learning that war and yet more terrible war is normal, not an aberrant disaster" (p. 113). During the war episode (which makes up the bulk of the autobiography), the False Parents appear frequently in caricature. The caricature is at times so strong that it is easy to dismiss its subject as social or political rather than internal and, consequently, part of that "normal", ever-continuing warfare. There is, for example, the genteel old lady at the Cheltenham tea-party who finally gets Bion into a corner on his own to put her prize question: "What was it like when you drove your tank over *people*?" She is associated, in the context of the book, with "Mother England, that old whore" who "crucifies" her sons (pp. 265–266).[2] There is the Church with its heart-warming stories of soldiers who make the best of the loss of a leg through philosophical observations about "only having one boot to clean now". There is the Major who sends him on suicidal missions with the fake parental concern of "Don't risk the lives of your men", backed by the cosy glow of exclusive man-to-man talks: "Doesn't do to have these chaps [i.e., non-commissioned officers, the lower orders] hanging around when we have secret stuff to discuss. Now, tell me, what was it like?" (p. 141). Like the Cheltenham lady, he displays the obscene curiosity that is sanctioned and encouraged by impeccable "etiquette".

Death itself becomes a "crisis of etiquette" when Smith becomes "It" and his rigid limbs refuse to be forced into their shallow grave. Instead of shocking the soldiering schoolboys into contact with emotional reality, the continuous degrading confrontation with actual death serves to reinforce the "sense of unreality": "I was shocked [to find an acquaintance just killed]. I was shocked to find I didn't care". At one point, Bion describes the Dantesque groans of unsalvageable wounded men stuck in the mud where stretcher-bearers dared not reach them: "Like marsh birds, innumerable bitterns mating . . . not raucous or crude, gentle. Dante's Inferno—but how much better we do these things now". An officer curses the tortured internal babies: "Shut up! Shut up! you noisy sods, you bleeding pieces of Earth". Bion continues:

> But they didn't. And they don't. And still the warning voices sound in answer to the sufferers of bereavement, depression, anxiety. "Don't go off the beaten track. Don't do as the psycho-analysts do. Haven't you heard? Pay Stills Your Conscience Here. Don't go off

the beaten Church. Remember Simon Magnus. Leave Your mind alone. Don't go down the Unconscious Daddy: Let the Gold Mine come up to you." [p. 143]

Later in the war, when Bion is intimately confronted with death again, his internal reaction is the same attempt to deny emotional "ghosts". His runner, Sweeting, loses the left side of his chest and keeps imploring Bion: "Mother, Mother . . . You will write to my mother sir, won't you?" To which Bion's unspoken reply is "No, blast you, I shan't! Shut up! Can't you see I don't want to be disturbed? These old ghosts, they never die; they preserve their youth wonderfully . . . So, so . . . death-like, isn't it?" (p. 249). This was the day—8th August—on which Bion says he "died" (p. 265).

The claustrophobic "web of undirected menace" strangles genuine intelligence and emotional reality. There is, as Bion puts it, "no where to run" as the network of interlocking fears holds the individual fast. Success or failure within the system is unrelated to courage; himself recommended for a VC, "I might with equal relevance have been recommended for a Court Martial. It depended on the direction which one took when one ran away" (p. 278). Either way, the individual runs into the basic-assumption web. The web's definition of "intelligence" is brilliantly captured in Bion's hilarious account of a staff Intelligence Officer asking him, after a so-called "battle", "Did you notice when the alluvial changed to the cretaceous?" (p. 138). Here, in the autobiography, there is a suggestion of a mind–body metaphor which is more pronounced in the *Memoir*, in which different kinds of false protection (cretaceous, like the bony skull) for the vulnerable "alluvial" brains or minds are portrayed. Thus, Bion alludes later to the Intelligence Officer's question, with: "Certainly the ground was dry and chalky—was that what the intelligent fool called cretaceous? I hoped I was not going to see it change to the alluvial"—that is, see "brains bulge out" as in the *Memoir* (1991, p. 154). His comment on this "intelligence" system is that "No fool could have arranged the battle I had just seen for myself".

Conversely, it is a system in which any genuine intelligence requires to be squashed or outcast, thereby creating society's cripples. In the war, such "breakdown" is represented by "shell-shock"—those who were not killed, yet "not robust enough to get shellshock", simply "fading away" into safer jobs (1982, p. 236). Outside the war, there are figures such as the tragic Hirst, head of the prep-school, whose wife entered a lunatic asylum immediately after their marriage, a victim of the sexual intimidation which drove the pubescent "wiggling" Bion to watch out obsessively for "the first signs of insanity" (p. 78), and the child Bion to fears (and, indeed, actual threats) of being expelled, like "Adam and Eve from the Garden of Eden—by God or some archangel with his flaming sword" (p. 46). In the words of his own father: in a "just war, we must fight with clean hands" (p. 109).

Bion's childhood Garden of Eden was India, whose black and gold colours have superimposed on them the image of a "green hill", associated with his mother's lap and singing "There is a green hill far away" with his sister while their mother played the harmonium:

> The parched Indian landscape must have drained all its green into that hill, which retained its city wall like a crown within which were tiny spires and towers huddled together against the foes "without".

The image of the mother–hill has a certain ambiguity which puzzled the small child: "It took me a long time to realise that the wretched poet meant it had no city wall" (p. 9). Is it safe, or not? Are the children within, or "without" it—do they have it, or not? His mother's lap felt "warm and safe" at first, then suddenly "cold and frightening". His mother is also associated with luscious hats, like the one with clusters of grapes which earned her the title of "an abandoned woman" because she wore it to Church (p. 15); or the "millinery cake" hat which was Wilfred's last image of her, bobbing up and down the green hedge, when she abandoned him at his prep-school (p. 33).

The duality is part of the Big Brother system to which all seem helplessly subject: did she abandon him or he her? In what sense was she "abandoned" herself? Although the child can read her feelings in her face ("I felt she was laughing inside"), there is an unacknowledged embargo upon any genuine expression of feeling that makes his own emotions uncontainable. Thus, in the period before he is due to be sent away to school in England:

My mother just stroked my cheeks and dreamt without fear but with sadness. I couldn't stand it.

"Moth-er! You aren't sad are you?"

"Sad?" She would laugh. "Of course not! Why should I be sad?"

Well, why should she be sad? I couldn't think. It was ridiculous. Sad? Of course not! [p. 21]

The key phrase is "I couldn't think". Where there is no language for confronting emotion, thought is impossible. By considering her own feelings outcast, the mother is unable to contain and respond to the child's. The problem with his relationship with his father is different in so far as he only loved "his image" of the children to start with, not the actual children themselves; he is yet further removed from reality. The mother "knew she had two nasty brats and could tolerate that fact; my father bitterly resented the menace of any reality which imperilled his fiction". But it is similar, in that the non-communication on which it is based has an inkling of treachery, the same hot–cold feeling. On one occasion, his father "sat me kindly and patiently on his lap" while drawing from him a kind of confession about why he had hit his sister; as soon as the confession is drawn, "the storm burst" and the boy is beaten, resulting not even in pain, but rather in a blank vacancy: "'Oh God, not that!' I felt wordlessly, mindlessly" (p. 11). The beating, or rather the treachery, is the genesis of "Arf Arfer", the God/Father who induces mindless terror.

The problem of the suppression of emotional reality is linguistically expressed; or rather, Bion expresses how it was evaded: how "wordlessly" and "mindlessly" go together. The child mutters the nightly prayer "Pity my Simply City" with his eyes "fixed" on his father's watch chain (p. 13), as if on the mystery of his father's glittering sexuality, which is also suggested by the "Electric City" train that is in turn linked by the child, linguistically and mentally, with the imaginary City on the Green Hill, thereby suggesting the male and female link he is trying to make in his mind. Yet his father, instead of helping the child push his fantasy through to the level of thought, negates as evidence of stupidity the metaphorical language which makes the child ask whether "Electric City" is "green like the other one". In itself this seems to comply with the denial of sexuality imposed by the "web of menace" and reinforced by the particularly rigid, puritanical standards of the household—

associated, it seems, with ambivalence about the mother's Anglo-Indian identity and with the father's missionary background. Wilfred's parents took great pains and went to some sacrifice to encourage educational ideas and procure toys on the right lines (such as buying him an electric train); but they were "afraid I would 'get ideas' if I were allowed to have contact with any kind of 'pagan superstition' at variance with the pure, unsullied belief of our puritan and their missionary forbears" (p. 15). The household is geared against the kind of sexuality that is implied in "getting ideas"—the marriage of sexes, cultures, dream and daytime, fact and metaphor. Wilfred learns to stop asking questions, to keep his mouth shut, and to become adept at lying, at presenting an appearance. It is because the superficial good behaviour, or "not lying", is, in fact, a "lie in the soul" at a deep level that Wilfred is so guilty and his father so furious when, during the episode of the flower-arrangement, he insists that he is not lying in claiming this image of his mother as all his own work (pp. 12, 34).

Meanwhile, the child's sexuality develops as it were illicitly in his relation with his mother, who is in part an "abandoned woman" with her love stronger than her pride. It is as if his mother's secret strain of Indian blood were a key to the secret of his parents' sexuality and also to the prototype of sado-masochistic war between male and female, in which Wilfred's concept of masculinity seems to develop antithetically to his father's. The father is, as well as a "brilliant engineer", a "noted Big Game shot", a successful hunter, and the conflict between father and son is epitomized on the day of a Big Game Hunt which is also Wilfred's birthday and the day of the presentation of the electric train. This combination suggests the parents' hope of developing the child in some sense in his father's footsteps. However, the train proves faulty, which not only disappoints but humiliates the father (as he is later humiliated by Wilfred's rejection for the Army); and further, enrages him when Wilfred does not identify with his own scientific means of reparation, but instead with the superstition of the Indian bearer, who smothers the train with ghee and leaves it to melt in the sun. The result is that "Arf Arfer with his great black wings beating had already obscured the sun" (p. 17).

Likewise, in the hunt, the child identifies with the hunted rather than the hunter. At night he becomes the prey of the female tiger whose mate has been shot, and, frightened rather than made self-righteous by tales of the Indian Mutiny, he feels himself a "little white brat" liable to die of fright like the Indian who dropped dead when confronted by "Nickel Sehn" of the Master Race. By a parallel process, his sister with her goggle-eyed parrot also becomes a night-time tormentor: "Arf Arfer had come! With his great goggle eyes and bright painted visage" (pp. 27–29). The implications of this network of images are further heightened in the *Memoir*, when the tormented cat in the otter hunt episode turns on its tormentors in their dreams and becomes the Great Cat Ra, a "Tiger Tiger burning bright / In the forests of the night" (Bion, 1991, p. 441). The Cat is Ra, in distinction to Raj and in reversal of Arf. In Bion's childhood, the gun wielded by the great white hunters receives a sinister reply in the image of the carved Indian god that Wilfred is taken to see at Gwalior: "the black more intense and forbidding because the brilliant sun made the shadows so harsh. I was afraid. Was the Indian ruler like that? I didn't want to go further into Gwalior" (1982, p. 32).

Later, the image of this black idol in the sun is echoed in Bion's staring at a Lewis gun, also silent in the sun, sweating with terror, and in his first confrontation with a First World War tank astride the road (pp. 201, 115). And the relation between the sexes, like that between the cultures, seems a kind of Tiger Trap in which it is hard to distinguish who is trapping, seducing, hunting whom. The child Wilfred resorts instead to "wiggling" and to being, rather than playing with, locomotives: "Before I had time to think I was racing around ... the Devil had entered into me" (p. 29). It is a kind of identification that, again, pre-empts thought: action which does not allow for "time to think". He finds India a "marvellous place to play trains", enacting a version of his father's "engineering" which inevitably conjures up Arf Arfer and revenge: "Whoever was that screaming?" (pp. 22, 37).

Wilfred's immediate reaction to abandonment by his mother in the prep-school playground is to be "numbed, stupefied". And again, before he has "time to think", he is forced straight away to take sides: to partake in the current group warfare and declare his allegiance to A or B (p. 33). These events (or event) set the pattern for his school existence. His mother becomes a figure who is, as it were, unthinkable in the context of school—as is India, with the richness of its Garden of Eden significance. Thus, he refuses to take into school the chocolates which she offers in a Golden Syrup tin ("the container in Indian days for many of our luxuries"); he does not like to be reminded of his mother's existence by Mrs Rhodes; already the pain of home leave is intolerable. He gives up asking for the hymn "Summer suns are glowing", which is associated with India and with the yellow buttercups which recall his mother, when he feels humiliated by his teacher Miss Good (p. 41).

Some years later, the adolescent Bion is brought into touch with a "sense of loss"—a sense which, earlier, would have been unthinkable and unfeelable, like taking "home leave" without "anaesthetic" (p. 115). He achieves this emotional contact through his relationship with Colman, a master he admired, and who could comfort him "not by anything he said, but by what he was". Colman's integrity is reflected in the different kind of patriotism which he offers Wilfred through their exploration of the landscape of the Fens—the England of Ely Cathedral and Hereward the Wake: "I was dismayed, resentful, of a past so filled with renown that it both stimulated and imposed a dead hand on my inchoate ambitions" (p. 97). The sense of loss, though newly felt, derives, he knows, from earlier than the war. Like the significance of his lost mother, it seems to be associated with the knowledge of the failure to make emotional contact with the past riches of civilization: the England it is worth being patriotic over; India; or Virgil and Homer, for whom one master had that rare quality, a genuine passion. Yet awareness of the renowned past, the rich inheritance of pioneering parents, is—like sex—frustrating because not truly cultivated by society; it "stimulates" while simultaneously "imposing a dead hand". Colman himself was subject to crippling headaches which would send him "dazed and almost reeling" out of the class—not quite to the "looney bin" or state of "shellshock", but certainly on related lines (p. 100).

Bion himself makes every effort to avoid such pain and frustration; throughout his school days he shied off learning anything, owing to a sort of nameless dread of home leave. There is, for example, his pert rebuffal of the classics master, who had a genuine passion for his subject, and who was annoyed and puzzled by Wilfred's refusal to engage in learning with any enthusiasm or emotional commitment. Bion, who excelled at sports that did not

involve a "hard object" such as a bat, says he came nearer to playing the game "for the sake of the game" than to working "for the
sake of work" (p. 93). Yet in the autobiography there is a key
description of a Run, which seems to symbolize a race against
himself—an attempt to win at all costs. Bion's only serious opponent in the race is an athlete who is favoured by the classics master
and who is, therefore, associated with the kind of scholarship of
which Bion is not only jealous and envious, but terrified: scholarship which stimulates emotional roots and arouses "inchoate ambitions". The sinister nature of the Run as he describes it, and his
terror of his opponent, figures his own endeavour to keep down,
win against, any activity which gets too close to emotional involve-
ment; he runs not for the sake of the run, but in order to prove
his self-mastery by fulfilling the category of "winning" (pp. 94–97).

The general nature of school games was as a "prelude to war";
and the Run shows that this applied not only to team games.
Likewise, Wilfred was a "conscript ally" in the "warfare" of young
Rhodes and Hamilton with their families; likewise, he learnt to
become adept at "lying" in the general moral or religious warfare.
He describes how the small boy "fires off moral grapeshot like 'I
haven't done anything!' before there is time for the adult to formulate a charge"; the adult then "fires an equally polyvalent
forgiveness" (p. 48). The "high moral tone" of the school was preserved by the careful supervision of its "gigantic sexual pressure
cooker" by the "big guns"—two or three masters of "unimpeach-
able integrity"; the big guns would "come into action" by "loosing
off only small-arms ammunition in the form of a cosy sexual talk"
(pp. 77–79). Prayer Meetings are another form of games-like
evasion ("Price went in to bat first . . ."), and Wilfred floats in
and out of them, continually disappointed with the effectiveness of
religion as a regulator of sexual desires.

Outside the school itself, his two main alternative homes are the
Rhodes and the Hamilton households. At the Rhodes', he seems to
find a sort of readymade warfare in the animal ruthlessness of the
farmer's attitude to the "facts of life", which is pierced only by the
figure of Kathleen, who is considered by the boys to be "wet" but
by Bion to embody genuine courage, as she is capable of voicing the
unspeakable truth. He admits, however, that he did not quite have
the courage to be in love with her, but only in love "in my fashion

. . . provided it did not cost too much" (p. 62). At the Hamiltons', life is more cultured, so the boys have to invent games which act out the theme of destruction of the mother's body or raiding its secret hideout. Such games are the otter hunt (retold in the *Memoir*), the toy soldiers, and the trench dugout in the orchard: "explosive experiments in warfare, aeronautics and cookery", with the makeshift aeroplane prefiguring the actual tank in the war. In the midst of this, Mrs Hamilton, who is a kind of foster-mother in fact adored by the young Wilfred, is generally agreed to have "lost her nerve":

> The deterioration in Mrs. Hamilton's sense of humour and Dudley's augmentation of his capacity for secrecy proceeded on parallel but non-Euclidean lines which sloped to terminate in an 18 inch balustrade between us and the garden some 30 feet below. [p. 72]

Bion's adolescence was by no means starved of good parental figures, but the duality which bound them all in the "web of menace" somehow contributed to his failure to internalize an endoskeleton. The structures to which he entrusted his mind were as fragile as the home-built aeroplane that seemed so imposing to the boys, yet nearly led to their death.

As if fulfilling the predestined pattern set by his experiences thus far, Bion explains that he "had applied to go to Tanks as it was the only way to penetrate the secrecy surrounding them". His first sight of a tank at the Training Camp evokes primitive sinister fears associated with the false image of the mother's body, secret rather than private. The description recalls the tiger trap of Gwalior, and prefigures the charred bodies of his crew as he sees them later in the war, hanging out of their burning tank like entrails.

> I saw my first tank—it blocked the road to camp. The day was hot, sunny, still. The queer mechanical shape, immobilised and immobilising, was frightening in the same way as the primitive tiger trap near Gwalior. I wanted to get away from it. A metallic hammering came from inside; a soldier got out and the day sprang into life again. [p. 115]

The hammering from within resulting in the soldier's emergence as part of a kind of birth process ("sprang into life"), is an example of the chick-hatching metaphor running throughout; later, Bion has pieces of tank adhering to him like pieces of shell (metallic or cretaceous). In the *Memoir*, the escape from the burning tank images the birth of thought itself.

There are other experiences of nameless dread during the war, reminiscent of the first viewing of the tank, when he is gripped by horror and dread, for which "even now I can find no words" (p. 237). They seem associated with the re-emergence of night-time terrors from his childhood in India, which now appear to be acted out in actuality. At the beginning of the war, he is kept "mercifully ignorant" by a "sense of unreality", and dissociated from the knowledge of his own fear—"which, for practical purposes, is as good as not being afraid". His innumerable narrow escapes from death pass unnoticed or as comic sequences. When fear does begin to erupt, Bion—recognizing that he is hemmed in and cannot run away ("in so far as such an expression is related to muscular activity", p. 146)—experiments with "enthusiasm" and "religion", only to find that these "take" less well than medical inoculation (p. 117). His description of receiving the DSO for the battle of Cambrai emphasizes the agony of unanaesthetized "home leave"; the renewed contact yet impossibility of emotional contact with his mother makes him feel he has "entered hell", and after this he notes an indefinable "change" in his attitude to the war (p. 201). The nameless dread presses more insistently on his imagination.

Thus, on the way back to the front, there is a curious episode in which, dozing behind a bank, he overhears what in England would pass as an "ordinary lovers-lane conversation" between a nurse and an officer. But to him, like Mrs Hamilton, "my nerve must have gone. I was petrified with fear". They are speaking about a wounded officer who, though not mortally wounded, nevertheless "snuffs it", owing to his delusions that "the Boche were after him" and that, moreover (extending the enemy), "the nurse was trying to murder him". Yet it appears that, in a sense, the officer's delusion is truer than actuality; the nurse *was* trying to murder him. Bion is told later that she is "a charmer"; it is as if she comes into his own nightmare as a prototype of the vengeful or aggressive Circean woman, the true enemy, luring and charming men to their death: "So; the officer had died of wounds . . . or was it shell-shock?" (p. 193). He died of his dream in which he watched the lawn open up and a woman walk out of it towards him "till he screamed!" It is part of a whole pattern of imagery associated with the Tiger and her revenge: there are traps, womb-graves, false births, imprisoned or mutilated foetuses, in a continuous pattern of mutual recrimination between "container" and "contained". The nightmare is inseparable from Bion's own attitude to the Tank and is at the root of his belief that he failed to be a "war hero" in a real sense.

After this Bion becomes more in touch with his own fear—as when the Tank seems to become the Tiger: "I was interrupted by fear, fear which became suddenly acute as the engine roared into life and at once settled into a gentle purr". Tool-making man, ambiguously "drawing on his brains", has invented a "machine-gun with a tougher skull, the tank" (p. 246). But "ghostridden" Bion and Hauser have to helplessly watch their tanks "purring on" to certain destruction:

> The whole four had flowered. Hard, bright flames, as if cut out of tinfoil, flickered and died, extinguished by the bright sun. One tank, crewless, went on to claw at the back of one in front as if preparatory to love-making; then stopped as if exhausted. [p. 254]

The tanks are primitive, female, Tigers, or (in a prehistoric capacity) Dinosaurs, whose revenge for their destruction is the spewing forth of the charred bodies of men from a ravaged womb, in a kind of terrifying primitive sado-masochistic ritual.

Several times in the later stages of the war, Bion has the sense of being a "cornered rat", the subject of a clumsy attempt at extermination by Arf Arfer, the Tiger, Lord Cat Almighty: "I had escaped— apparently. Who knew what Lord Cat Almighty was up to during this short respite?" (p. 262) It becomes clear that his fear is not of death as such, but of nightmare coming true: the fear of being the hunted animal under an evil spell. In the face of a total disintegration and splintering of personality, clumsily "clubbed to death", he resorts to mathematical exactitude and precision, to the "cabbalistic figures" of compass and map: "I started to take compass-bearings as my way of keeping fear at bay" (pp. 233, 243).

I have put this down precisely because it was the kind of precise nonsense we used, to give substance to a figment of the imagination . . . It is such a relief to know exactly where everyone is. When you have no idea where you are yourself it is, as I discovered, an admirable substitute. [p. 208]

His "topological enthusiasm" represented another attempt to keep fear at bay, to stop fear from swallowing him up, devoured by his own nightmare: "Watch the Head devour its Tale", as he puts it in the *Memoir* (p. 119). Bion writes that given the nature of a cruel and vengeful God, Jesus' cry on the cross might more rationally have been "My God, my God, why hast thou remembered me?" It is as if, "remembering" his own fear, he suddenly feels remembered by the Arf Arfer of his childhood, punished for the loss of his mother, which was nevertheless outside his "ghost-ridden" control.

Bion regards himself as already having "died" in spirit when, at the place named, absurdly, Happy Valley (at Sequehart), he evacuates himself and his crew from the tank, and sends the cretaceous "skull" on alone to destruction minus the vulnerable "brains" housed within it. A combination of 'flu and alcohol served to help save his life. In the *Memoir*, this episode becomes a description of inspired thought; here, it is more of primitive, impulsive action: "Before I knew what I was doing I had left the driver's seat" (1982, p. 262). In a strange way, after the period of nameless dread, he becomes dissociated from the war. The earlier action of the "sleep-walking" infantry who had refused to leave their trench, but simply watched the tanks "flowering", had "impressed my hidden reserves of intelligence" (pp. 254–256). The "sleepwalking" provides a kind of alternative to either disobedience to orders, or shellshock. It enables Bion to invent the technique that he calls "patrolling the enemy position", by means of a crewless tank going up and down until it got hit. It is as if some hidden part of himself managed to keep his body alive despite his emotional "death": the emotional death which occurred with Sweeting's appeal to mediate between his dead self and his mother: "You will write to my mother Sir won't you?"—"And then he died. Or perhaps it was only me" (pp. 249, 264).

Bion is left after the war with no idea of where he is himself; he has only, as it were, a series of map-references and compass-bearings, a "chitinous semblance" of a self, a great void between himself and his internal mother. He saw his survival as an internal disaster with which he was not equipped to cope, and in one sense devoted the rest of his life to trying to deal with his guilt. The factual auto-biography of *The Long Week-End* is complemented by the self-analytic fantasy of *A Memoir of The Future,* which relives the past of childhood and youth in the present, and stimulates the growth that could not take place at the time owing to the exo-skeletonous "web of menace" which held him in thrall. Indeed, not the least interest-ing aspect of *The Long Week-End* is the way it provides an introduc-tion to the *Memoir,* illuminating some of the obscurities of a private life and language with private reference points: Arf Arfer, the Tiger in the night, the otter hunt, the cornered rat, the pregnant child, the suicide in the pigeon cote, the "brain-fever" bird, and so on. Taken together, the external and the internal autobiography approach "the formulation of phenomena as close as possible to noumena"; providing a map of the human condition whose abstraction has live roots in realism.

## *All My Sins Remembered*

"Is there any desert such as a sojourn amongst non-combatants?" asks Bion, after describing how, for the first time since demobiliza-tion, he encounters someone who "recognizes" him, in the true sense of a reciprocal response to his human condition: "Bion!" he exclaimed with the relief—which was mutual—that must have been experienced when Crusoe and Man Friday met; like the shadow of a great rock in a thirsty land (Bion, 1985, p. 52).

"Bion" is somebody who actually exists. The simile recalls his last tank-crew, stumbling across the cretaceous bedrock in the shadow of a forty-ton tank, which Bion had been inspired to convert into a protector rather than a destroyer of life. Twenty years have gone by since then—the pre-war years—and now it is time for the next one. But this is not the first time in the book that he has mentioned an encounter with "figures from the past"—that is, from the first war. While in Oxford he had encountered "the poor Major" and, shortly afterwards, Quainton. But there is no emotional con-tact: the Major "cuts him dead" (p. 13), while Quainton and Bion observe each other through "a cold glazing of the eyes as if a thin film separated us and prevented what might have become a mutual hatred" (p. 14). In the *Memoir*, such thin but impenetrable films become a "diaphragm" of distrust between different parts of the personality, and it takes an artist like Picasso to present the picture from both sides of the glass plate.

A couple of pages later, in *Sins*, we hear of how Bion always "kept a glaze handy for slipping over [his] tell-tale eyes" (p. 16)— this time in the context of sexual indiscretion, when one of his old schoolmasters (now a colleague) inadvertently dropped a condom on the floor, then "smartly slid a slippered foot" over it to hide it from view. Bion's equivalently smartly-shuttered eyes indicate his social complicity in the mutual lie, but, at the same time, highlight his constrained observational capacities—his "tell-tale eyes". Later, in the context of medical training, he sees himself in the "central position of the fool" (p. 37), and at one point he notices a needle (which turns out to be a piece of bloodstained thread) left lying in the wound, and finds his voice—despite himself—drawing attention to this uncomfortable fact:

> What a funny voice! Who is that talking in the theatre? That bloody fool again?
> "Sir, there's a needle lying in the wound." Such a queer voice.
> "Needle? Where?" Not at all funny voice—angry. [pp. 40–41]

The inner voice comes from outside conscious control, speaking up despite his fear of appearing a fool. A hidden part of himself (perhaps the Elephant's Child), detecting an emergency, made use of his phonation.[3] The thread proved both that he was a "fool" in one sense (p. 43), yet also that his fool-ish, truth-seeing eyes windowed an innate perceptiveness thirsty for reciprocation in the desert of his post-war self.

As already suggested by the school episode, this is inseparable from the question of sexuality, which now becomes the focus of his struggle to develop his inner "substance" and to throw off the "chitinous semblance" of a human being that veiled his inner spark of sincerity after the war. For "If I, as I hoped, was a person of substance, I had not so far discovered any substance of which I should be glad to be composed" (p. 42). Despite the lack of sexual experience that he affirms, all encounters and combinations described are inherently sexual. They range from the perversity of the charge of paedophilia at his old school to the happy "hetero-sexual, homo-sexual, gastronomic love" he has for his cousins (p. 43). That "explains everything—except to me", he writes. Of course, nothing is explained; it is just described, and so we can trace the underlying pattern of the relationships, both real and unreal. Sexuality, as is made most clear in the *Memoir*, applies not only to interpersonal relationships (male–female, boy–man, child–parents, etc.), but to many other types of caesural meeting where a creative mingling of vertices is required for thought to germinate: such as Psyche–Soma, ugly–beautiful, or pre- and post-natal. It is for this reason (rather than the strictly Freudian) that sexuality is the basis of psychoanalytic thinking.

The development of his sexuality is thus co-extensive with the development of his interest in psychoanalysis. It begins with his urge to help "restore the wounds" of both the Major and Quain-ton; despite their submerged mutual hostility, "I wished I could help [Quainton] as some small way of being grateful" for his "cheerfulness" at Ypres. Bion recognized intuitively that his personal salvation was inseparable from this spontaneous urge to help his war comrades, whether or not he was capable of helping or they of being helped. Indeed, he always saw psychoanalysis as a relationship of mutual assistance, rather than one of moralistic correction. It was always the "bad jobs", such as psychoanalysis, that "made some sense of me" (p. 61). He was "made" but not "born" a psychoanalyst, he said (p. 49)—it was a struggle. Luckily, by contrast with trying to become a poet if you were not born one, it was at least possible.[4] In any case, psychoanalysis was being made at the same time, and was still in its "fumbling infancy" (1991, p. 130). But, as he said of his analysis with Melanie Klein (1985, p. 68), and as with other forms of non-dreadful sexuality, it did require reciprocation.

For after eighty years' experience, says Bion, he came to regard "sexual dread"—associated with war nightmares—as "indistin-guishable from dreadful sex" (p. 22), whether consummated or not. One such dreadful episode was the humiliation resulting from rejection by the girl who (he believed) took him for a glamorous war hero and then realized her mistake.

She took on a ready-made hero (certified genuine and authoritatively guaranteed) without the toil of discovering who or what *he* was. *He* took on a ready-made cosmetically guaranteed beautiful person without the toil of discovering what, if any, difference there is between a boy and a girl, a wife and a girl, a husband and a boy, a wife and a mother, or a husband and a father. [p. 30]

It was, from the start, a non-relationship between his own "war-hero trapping" ("hero dress" as he calls it in the *Memoir*) and her external beauty. Their inner selves were left out of the transaction. In a small snatch of dialogue he finds himself blurting out the words "perfectly priceless", and then, to explain the oddity of his remark, "I nodded speechlessly to her dress" (p. 18). It would have been a miserable match of "ectodermal proliferations" (to borrow a phrase from the *Memoir*) had it ever taken place—a classic respectable lie. Nonetheless, when her saner—if spiteful—hostility surfaces, it grates bitterly on him, since for a period no more genuine intimate relationship exists to take its place and reinforce his real endo-skeletal identity.

Another analogous episode, this time in connection with his move towards being "made" a psychoanalyst, was the caricature of an analysis undertaken with Dr FiP (Feel-it-in-the-Past). There was no reciprocation here either—neither between analyst and analysand, nor between the analysand and his real feelings. He could not feel it in the past; for "anything I felt, I *felt* in the present" (p. 42). *"What were your feelings?"* he asks himself, and this is the point at which he recounts a "glorious day of freedom" with his cousins. Yes—in such a context, he *did* have feelings. The Dr FiP experience, or non-experience, turned out to be an attempted seduction into mutual parasitism—another nightmare of perversity, perpetuated by the doctor being "a kindly man" who "allowed [Bion] to accumulate a debt" (p. 34). It was a case of "Don't go down the Unconscious, Daddy: let the Gold Mine come up to you!", as in *The Long Week-End*. But it required conduct that was *generally acknowledged* as unethical (fee-splitting) for Bion to realize he had been trapped in a false situation, another tank of respectable appearances, like the war. Its main contribution to Bion's learning from experience was to clarify the falseness of the (perennially popular) view of causality, in which the function of psychoanalysis is taken to be one of dredging up some repressed past trauma so that it can then be discarded in a quick "cure". "There is a kind of mad logic about it which was peculiarly convincing", he says (p. 35). But, after Dr FiP, Bion was adamant that "remembering" is not a process of rubbish disposal, but rather of seeking out the present life of feeling—the "true voice of feeling" as Keats calls it: the spark of sincerity that may be fanned into a flame. The past must be present-ed, as in the title of Book 2 of the *Memoir*.

The underlying pattern of *Sins*, as of all the autobiographical books, is thus the warfare between the real self with its potential germ of thought, and the mask which paralyses or thwarts its growth. "From that warfare there is no release", as he quotes several times in the *Memoir*.

> Blood says: this is true
> And that's but a mask.
> [Harris, "I ask a fresh vision", unpublished]

It sounds simple, even fool-ish; but it is the key to the whole psychoanalytic business and to every art-science that demands internal observation. At the heart of Bion's remembering is the recognition that "no amount of official certification by the highest authorities is any more use than the first aid bandage slung across the gap where Kitching's chest wall should have been" (Bion, 1985, p. 44).[5] Kitching's heart beating away his life epitomizes the vital spark of sincerity being extinguished. This and other war metaphors for mental life recur during Bion's medical training in London, where, for the first time (by contrast with Oxford University), he feels at home and "more nearly in my class" (p. 20). Outside the official arena of courtship and mate-hunting, other types of sexual education were taking place that were genuinely mind-building. Opportunities occur for learning how to distinguish between the spark of life-giving sincerity and the false exo-skeletal armour which prevents a "sexual" relationship between "growth-stimulating objects".[6]

Particularly vivid is the contrast presented by two of the chief surgeons with whom he trained—both "brilliant, world-famous technicians" but with quite different attitudes to the human material on which they operated. Julian Taylor had an unmatched technical brilliance but regarded the patient as having no worthwhile knowledge of himself or his body, simply because he was ignorant of medical diagnosis. Wilfred Trotter on the other hand, "listened with unassumed interest as if the patient's contributions flowed from the fount of knowledge itself. It took me years of experience before I learned that this was in fact the case" (p. 38). Trotter, owing to being in touch with his own ignorance of each patient as an individual, was capable of making a direct intuitive link with the core of their personality, their innate humanness. He could learn from the patient, not merely deliver expertise. This meant that his skin grafts "took" and were not rejected—they were sewn not just with needles, but with some ineffable growth potion like the Shakespearean *moly*; whereas Taylor's mechanically-applied grafts were "sloughed off" despite their technical mastery. Taylor's surgery was like the type of marriage that Bion summarizes in the following terms, referring to the case of a single mother who had been deserted by her husband: "The operation had been properly, technically performed. They were married in Church, but the marriage did not take, so now—no bed yet" (p. 38).

Trotter, by contrast, knew about real marriage in the surgical setting. He knew how to make contact with the Platonic "fount of knowledge" that resided in that particular patient; just as, years later, Bion realized the analytic patient was the one person who could give the analyst genuine assistance.[7] The equivalence of blood and vital spirit became more than metaphor. Bion learnt from watching these men about the communication necessary between Soma and Psyche, as described in the *Memoir*. "Years of experience" later, he understood the nature of what he learnt embryonically at that time.

The primary influence of Trotter on Bion was not *Instincts of the Herd in Peace and War* (1916), but his evocation of love in his student—the opposite of the paedophilia of which Bion had himself been accused as a young schoolmaster. It was the kind of love for an inspired teacher that metamorphoses into the qualities of an internal object and thus engenders hope and self-respect. Bion "loved" Trotter, who is mentioned in the same breath as his cousins; referring to the episode of the thread, he writes: "Trotter could not possibly help knowing I was a fool, but he was able to respect my feelings. I loved Marguerite and Herbert and Arnold and Trotter though I could never have dared to admit it" (p. 43). To "admit" love would require a further advance in genuine courage (as with Wilfred's admiration for Kathleen in *The Long Week-End*), but, nonetheless, the seeds had been sown. The sensitive educational environment provided by Trotter (by contrast with that of the army) had allowed Bion the courage to speak out, however "foolishly" (but not entirely) mistaken he may have been in his interpretation of the evidence of his tell-tale eyes. It was only a blood-stained thread, not a needle, in the wound—but who could be certain until it was picked out? If "even Trotter made mistakes" (p. 40) then so could he, Bion, without sinking into the puritanical conformist, non-conformist abyss of self-loathing.

As with the Rhodes and Hamiltons in *The Long Week-End*, this was an aspect of education "not in the timetable", and that contributed to his future ability to become both a lover and a psychoanalyst. Trotter's handling of his patients helps Bion (in a way that he could not himself help Quainton) to heal the war's nightmares:

> I remember the near horror with which I saw him enter a skull with powerful blows of a mallet on the chisel he held. Such was his control that he could and did penetrate the hard bone and arrest the chisel so that it in no way injured the soft tissue of the underlying brain. [p. 37]

This account rewrites the memory of the skull-crushing monsters (of the *Memoir*) and their progenitors, the tanks and snipers ("I hope it will be a good shot through the forehead and out with the brains at the back . . ."). Trotter could judge the boundary between the alluvial and the cretaceous. Hence for Bion, Trotter's "strong hands [had] a beauty which could not by any stretch of the imagination be regarded as the product of a manicurist's cosmetic skill" (1985, p. 37). From the strong but sensitive way Trotter "enters a skull" he learns (or relearns) what constitutes real beauty: as distinct from a "cosmetically guaranteed beautiful person" who is mistaken for a suitable sexual partner, or the "cosmetic qualifications" of the beautiful anaesthetist responsible for the death of a child on the operating table (p. 40), or the grotesque sexual caricature of the tanks "clawing at each other as if preparatory to lovemaking" in *The Long Week-End*.

Trotter could be a "bad tempered man" when engaged in a difficult operation, because he cared about the outcome (p. 40), whereas

Dr FiP was a "kindly person" but had no interest in nurturing life, merely in being comfortable. This sort of keenly-observed contrast taught Bion—or reminded him—that it is the turbulent experience of Love, Hate, and Knowledge that is real; minus LHK is a matter of cosmetics. Yet in another sense Bion, through the act of narrative, is revealing to himself that what Trotter taught him about respect for life was only fully learnt some time after the surgical demon-stration, when it was "Too late, too late" (as the brain-fever bird called in his Indian childhood). He asks himself:

> Do you think, Mr Trotter, that I have to know what I am talking about? Do you think I might find a girl who would want to be married to me? And be a parent to our children? She might think I was brave; on the other hand she might not, and I don't like that much. [p. 39]

The above lines are a kind of dream; they come after a reference to *Hamlet*: "But if I go to sleep what dreams may come? Who is to be sure that they are only dreams?" In *Hamlet* it is Ophelia whom Hamlet accuses of cosmetic beauty intended to trap and deceive. Now Bion asks himself whether his autobiography is "truth? Or cosmetically acceptable fiction?" (p. 38). There is something else he has to inwardly question regarding his mode of remembering, bear-ing at the back of his mind Hamlet's words after the "To be or not to be" speech, when Ophelia enters his meditations: "Nymph, in thy orisons be all my sins remember'd" (quoted on p. 70).

For, despite Trotter's lessons in sexual love, Bion felt that he abandoned his first wife, Betty, when in 1939 he dumbly obeyed the old call to "glory" (p. 44) and left her, nearing the term of her preg-nancy, for the war. Remembering his experience of Trotter leads directly to thoughts of Betty. "I didn't know", he says, that she would die in childbirth: "I didn't know—no, but I should have known" (p. 39). Why should he have known? No external inter-preter could have accused him of any irresponsibility or lack of foresight—quite the contrary; there was even the fund of £8000 for Betty in the event of his death from being brave. And indeed, we can see that in external terms he tried not to be posted abroad. But his internalization of Trotter, with his acute somatic sensitivity to the delicate brains housed inside the skull, made him accuse himself. At some deep level, he could detect what was invisible to all eyes else—some falsification aroused by the war-drums and the obsession with "couvre-toi de gloire", a vestigial remnant of the desire to "win", as in the School Run. This Elephant's Child for once refrained from asking questions of himself—the only person who could answer them.

In view of what he experienced as a sort of internal, unintentional treachery, in retrospect he condemned his apparently responsible precautions on departure as a "cosmetically acceptable fiction". It was not the fact that he had to go; it was the fact that, internally, he was marching to the wrong tune, deaf to his own feelings:

> What killed Betty and nearly killed her baby? Physical malformation? Incompetent obstetrics? Callous or indifferent authorities? Or the revelations of the hollow nature of the masculine drum that was being so loudly beaten by her husband's departure? Or was there something false about the psychiatric tones, the psychiatric pressure waves that were being set up? How would a sensitive conductor feel if God or Fate or the Devil condemned him to an eternity of eliciting a harmonious response from a tone-deaf, malicious, instrumentally armed orchestra? [p. 62]

He knew—but he only got in touch with his knowledge afterwards. And what he learnt was not the literal truth, which by then was irrelevant, but the internal truth, the "marks made now" on his consciousness. The veil came down over his tell-tale eyes again, this time to hide the truth from himself, not others. But the cover was a cosmetic field-dressing. The picture of Betty as the troops depart, "white-faced" even against snow-clad Bournemouth, comes to haunt him like that of Sweeting with the blood draining from his heart. "You will write to my mother, Sir" transmutes into "Betty had to make her last journey on her own" (p. 60).

He gained relief later from Mrs Klein's apparent obliviousness to the glory of the DSO—symbol of the "cosmetic cover for cowardice" that obscured his knowledge of his own real feelings (p. 67). Unlike John Rickman, his second analyst (whose interpretations at least "reminded him of real life" [p. 46]), she had no interest in warfare other than the internal sort, and was "not easily led away from her awareness of a universe that is not subject to the needs and wishes of human beings"—that is, she had a strong sense of reality and was not impressed by decorations. Bion's narrative ends with an account of how he was forced by a cruel spark of sincerity to overcome the cowardly temptation to remain content with his post-war life—cottage, baby, nursemaid, bus service, even an income from his psychoanalytic practice. It made a "nice change from the Third Battle of Wipers" (to borrow his phrase from the *Memoir*, 1991, p. 577). The concluding episode, in which he refuses to pick up the baby who refused to crawl towards him, images his own painful emotional recognition of the need to seek another wife,[8] despite his resistance to being "reminded" of either Betty or the girl who had turned him down (1985, p. 69). Reflected in his "cruelty" to the child (p. 70) was the cruelty his internal objects were aiming at himself: piercing his "sense of gratification" by uncomfortable thoughts of love and sex—by a return to the real life of feeling, synonymous with the process of thinking itself.[9] It was no use—"all this gratifying world now began to be invaded by thought . . . The invasion could not be repelled or contained" (p. 66). An internal dialogue brings to his attention the need to "work at both ends":

> And how do I think anyway?
> *Sorry sir. I'll just put it down to your daughter . . . she's too young to mind anyway.*
> Here, half a minute. . . . How can I wag my vestigial tail when I am made to think? Obviously—work at both ends, below and above the umbilicus, caudal and cranial. [p. 65]

Bion's self-analysis had begun. Like his baby daughter, he had to get off his bottom and start crawling: tail and cranium co-operating on both sides of the diaphragm. He was on track for the thought "invasion" of the Empire of the Mind, which was to be depicted representatively in the "artificial dream" of the *Memoir of the Future*.

## Aftersong

> And I include all, even of the enemy,
> I looked into my heart as comrades,
> Let orders say what they will to regulate
> Hate: few, but some I found, men and women
> To love as comrades.

This too people at home find hard to realise,
Cannot believe coming back is not pure joy.
But more than all the fear of warfare
Is the fear in my heart of the loss
Of the love of comrades.

How the sky burned, and trees were fantastic,
And silhouettes of grim houses burning,
The hornet thrum of tyres, the thunder of
Armour, the reeling men and bridges;
The comrades I never knew!

I set these in images for my mind to remember,
Such false figures in images of possession.
For it is not excitement and danger
That are remembered passionately,
It is the love of comrades.

O young men! O young comrades!
Then is alive, and no past history,
And heart's is more intense tranquillity
Than folio's, knowing it can never now
Lose the love of comrades.
                    [Harris, "Aftersong", unpublished][10]

Bion's autobiographies, like my father's war poems, were written with a sense of mission—not so much to record as to create an
internal record, by means of "folio" (words on paper). The "false
figures"[11] refer to the garish metaphorical clothing of places, events,
people, which are necessary to hold the emotional meaning in the
process of expression and transcription. Bion said the same of his
recording of the external features of his own life—they are necessary, but irrelevant. The colourful images of burning trees and
houses are what Plato, in the *Phaedrus*, calls "aids to the recollection
of reality"; like Bion's dinosaur-tanks mating, they encapsulate an
emotional experience, giving it a local habitation and a name.
Coming back to oneself is not pure joy. But folio transcription, as is
traditional, enables an otherwise fugitive love to be preserved alive
in "intense tranquillity", not merely become "past history". The
"mark" that is left when "I write about me" gives substance to what
had seemed to be a mere "chitinous semblance" of a self, a cosmetic

disguise. The self is recreated in the telling and again with each reading that is an "emotional experience". It leaves its mark *now*— at the point of LHK—the point at which the noumenon of truthfulness "intersects with the human intelligence" (Bion, 1973–1974, Vol. II, p. 30). Such a story has the spark of sincerity, fuelled by a love it can never lose: for Sweeting, Betty, all the "young men", including the enemy and those who were never known;[12] and this journey is its own reward.

## Notes

1. This was the first review of his autobiography to be published.
2. "Miss Whybrow", who asks these anti-questions, is mentioned as "Myth Whybrow" in the *Memoir* (1991, p. 571) and glossed in the *Key* as a figure who represents the "inhibition of curiosity" (p. 675), the blind eye turned by the adult world to the child's questions.
3. Bion describes a patient who stammered as "making use of my phonation" (1977, p. 18).
4. Bion says here that Robert Bridges, the Poet Laureate, had to "discover" the fact that poets had to be born, not made.
5. Kitching is renamed Sweeting in *The Long Week-End* and the *Memoir*.
6. Bion's phrase from *Attention and Intepretation* (1970, p. 129).
7. As he puts it in *Taming Wild Thoughts*, the analysand is "both the person who presents himself for assistance and the person to whom we look for the most powerful assistance we are ever likely to find" (1997, p. 35).
8. An internal need inseparable from his own development; not merely the external practical need which, as he says, was obvious—"I did not need a psycho-analyst to tell me that" (Bion, 1985, p. 69).
9. I discuss this in *The Aesthetic Development* (Williams, 2010), to the effect that, despite Bion's self-castigation, it reads as an unconscious attempt to stimulate growth in both himself and the child, in the context of a comforting mummy-figure also being present to counterbalance the "cruelty". In actuality, it did not result in "losing his child", as we know from the preceding chapter (chronologically later), in which the child, now older, walks to meet him at the bus-stop: "At last the perilous ten yards would be achieved and tiny arms strove to meet around my neck" (Bion, 1985, p. 66).

10. A poem written after the Second World War. Roland Harris, my father (1919–1969), was an analysand of Bion's until he left for California, and was probably influential in encouraging Bion's venture into fiction in the *Memoir*.

11. "Figures" is a term from traditional rhetoric, referring to the expansion of meaning through metaphorical and grammatical patterns, as in "figures of speech".

12. As in Wilfred Owen's "I am the enemy you killed, my friend" ("Strange meeting"); see Bion's dialogue between Roland and Du in the *Memoir*.

# CHAPTER TWO

# Counterdreaming: *A Memoir of the Future*

> Time present and time past
> Are both perhaps contained in time future,
> And time future contained in time past.
> If all time is eternally present
> All time is unredeemable.
>
> (T. S. Eliot, "Burnt Norton", ll. 1–5)[1]

In previous essays, many years ago, I approached the *Memoir* first from the point of view of its "underlying pattern" as a literary work, and then, after the publication of *The Long Week-End*, with a view to selecting key episodes from each type of autobiography that could illuminate one another: in particular, the Tiger Hunt and its converse, the Tank of the war, with its graphic representation of dinosaur mentality.[2] Following this, I wrote the script of a film with Kumar Shahani in which the figure of Bion's Ayah was predominant;[3] later again, in the context of a search for Bion's "muse", I returned to this near-silent but significant feature of the autobiographies in the form of a verse-narrative spoken by the Ayah-as-goddess.[4]

In the present chapter, I would like to combine aspects of all these approaches to the *Memoir*, but most fundamentally, to return to my initial interest in the author's quest for formal structure, since I believe that for many readers a major obstacle to enjoying the *Memoir* is not the dream-content, but rather, a lack of generic reference-points. As Bion says elsewhere, "As a psycho-analyst I have been taught a good deal about the interpretation of dreams. The only thing I am not quite clear about is, what was the dream?" (Bion, 2005b, p. 46).

In other words, what kind of book is this? How does it work, how can we read it? Until this is answered—in the sense of demonstrated—we cannot make proper contact with the real shape or "underlying pattern" of the group that comprises this particular individual, and we cannot identify with the noumenon beyond the phenomena. It is not our interpretive powers but our observational ones that need to be marshalled, so we can set our receptivity in order by finding some form of symbolic congruence. Truth, including autobiographical truth, cannot be possessed or represented in any paraphraseable way but depends on a complex alliance of identification and aesthetic form; this applies to both reader and writer. It is not enough to see in the *Memoir* a mixture of dream-poem, Socratic dialogue, Shavian or Beckettian drama, Orwellian or Dodgsonian parable, and "pornographic novel" (as Bion described his intention).[5] What we need to know about the genre is something slightly different: not its literary roots, but its way of talking to us and engaging our attention. As Bion said of *The Long Week-End*, "if I could have resorted to abstractions I would have done so". The same applies here; by looking at a limited number of episodes linked across the three volumes we can see the "pattern underlying all the examples" (1991, p. 533)—the abstract thinking process itself.

At the same time, it is probably necessary to state what is true of all literary criticism, but perhaps especially of readings of autobiography:[6] that the following exposition constitutes my own dream of Bion's dream, so is, like psychoanalysis itself, a form of conversation with internal objects.[7] Like any reading which involves an "emotional experience of reading" (as Bion emphasized) the work becomes a caesura, like a piece of glass that can "be seen from both sides of the screen—both sides of the resistance" (Bion, 1991, p. 465).

## *The genre*

Bion describes the *Memoir* as a "fictitious account of psycho-analysis" (p. 4). It is not psychoanalysis (the "thing-in-itself"), but neither does he wish it to be just "talking about" psychoanalysis—a mode which he considers boring at best, lying at worst. The genre for such a "fictitious account", however, does not exist until the search begins: "I have to manufacture the apparatus as I proceed. I claim that it is artistic though the art has not yet been created . . ." (p. 88). It comes into being with its subject, the embryonic idea whose growth is overseen by internal objects. In my fantasy of the Ayah's "Confessions" she speaks as the internal goddess who frames the story:

> What rough beast now, so clumsy and obscure,
> Slouches towards my sacred river banks
> To be born? All my knowledge I gave last time,
> Stretching the limits of my philosophy;
> How many more times must this container my body
> Distend in roughening involutions
> To provide a lodgement for an idea
> Beyond the reach of thought? Once again
> Pulsations cross some coarse irregularity
> In me, and without thinking my agents begin
> To weave their pearly web over its hideous
> Grit, and the thing is not concealed but grows
> Hugely, though tiny, and seizes my attention.
> [Williams, "Confessions", ll. 19–31][8]

The "Confessions" are based on implicit more than explicit features of the autobiographies; nonetheless, Bion does explicitly stress the ancient idea of Woman-as-beauty-as-fertility, "brooding on the vast abyss" (as Milton puts it, *Paradise Lost*, I: 21), containing the seeds of a host of future shapes and forms. This goddess-figure has, over the millennia, sensed the stirrings of individual souls in the womb of the mind. Like embryos, they demand a local habitation and a name in the mother-consciousness. Each soul or idea is the same in principle, yet each is idiosyncratic and (to paraphrase *Hamlet*) stretches the containing powers of internal objects beyond the reach of existing thought.

The genre of *A Memoir of the Future* belongs to the pioneering tradition in which an author's self-analysis or internal autobiography is co-extensive with the creation of a new genre for self-expression. It is "a reverie *now*", as Bion described the process of reviewing his analysis with Mrs Klein. What starts with an "artificially constructed dream" (Bion, 1991, p. 4) turns into a real dream, a present experience. He regards the book, he says, as an "instrument" for investigation, not as a means for enshrining dogma (p. 204). As in Milton's *Samson Agonistes* (from which the title of the second volume, *The Past Presented*, derives) the protagonist of a reverie of this type becomes the subject of

> restless thoughts, that like a deadly swarm
> Of hornets armed, no sooner found alone,
> But rush upon me thronging, and present
> Times past, what once I was, and what am now.
> [*Samson Agonistes*, ll. 19–22]

Like Milton, rather than like Eliot, Bion believed that time was internally redeemable through writing the dream; the heart can gain the "intense tranquillity" that means (in Harris's words) it "can never now / Lose the love of comrades". The eternal presented-ness of time in autobiographical writing is not a lament, but an opportunity for transformation—for "suffering a sea-change" as Shakespeare puts it (*The Tempest*, I.ii.: 403).

The "memory" of Bion's past life, or mind, with its succession of catastrophic changes, is reviewed in the present by a group of internal voices or characters, who are simultaneously previewing the significance of his "self" for the future. The characters represent different "vertices" of his thinking, and their significance lies in their links and tensions. They include a Priest; a Psychoanalyst; a pair of Dinosaurs; various biological Ages including pre-natal ones; a Voice which obtrudes from the somatic depths as from the Marabar caves, and ambiguously belongs to God or the Devil; Sherlock Holmes (a model for the practical investigator), his brother Mycroft, and their opponent Moriarty (Morality, the Devil himself);[9] various other figures from fiction, history or mythology; a microcosmic cross-section of Edwardian society in the form of Robin (the farmer–scientist), the upper-class couple Roland (farmer–sceptic) and Alice; their maid Rosemary, and "Neanderthal" worker Tom;

Ghosts from the war; Bion himself, and his alter-ego Myself. Some of these characters rotate on an axis "not different but reversed" as Bion puts it, such as: Priest and P.A.; Rosemary and Alice; Roland, Robin, and mysterious Man who represents the invading forces that turn the established order of English Farm upside down.[10] Man attempts to keep order by means of his automatic (or is it a chocolate bar?), yet is ultimately enmeshed in the "cloud drift" of thronging voices (Bion, 1991, p. 122),[11] and finds himself in thrall to Rosemary with her "dancing feet".

Fictional characters, says Bion, have always contributed greatly to the healthy operation of his mental digestive system. They enable him to use meta-phor (literally, transference)—the serviceability of "as if" (p. 216). They are, in fact, the "reversed perspective of the abstract" and, thus, enable the abstract to be deduced (p. 209) or, at least, "felt on the pulses" (as Keats would say). A fictional form is more responsive than theoretical language to aspects of truth that are trying to "get through" the impenetrable barrier of complacent knowing-about:

> P.A.: His Satanic Jargonieur took offence; on some pretence that psycho-analytic jargon was being eroded by eruptions of clarity. I was compelled to seek asylum in fiction. Disguised as fiction the truth occasionally slipped through. [p. 302]

Fiction provides a shelter from the barrage of basic assumptions, lies, and cant. Bion images this situation in terms of the soldier cowering in the "angle of the wall", seeking protection from the "white feathers" rained down by society or the bludgeoning of bullets within the psychoanalytical "dovecote".[12] Such bludgeon- ings are a later version of the "virulent, vigorous, overpowering culture of non-conformist Protestant cant" of his childhood, which he felt had thwarted the natural development of his sexuality (see Bion, 1985, p. 43). The angle of the wall is a nook in which the germ of an idea may take root and grow, outside the reach of "answers", "dogmas", and "scientific facts" (Bion, 1991, p. 239). Non-artistic methods (and projections) are "less accurate than those used by artists" (*ibid.*, p. 110).

Indeed the psychoanalytical dovecote is only the latest in a long line of historical institutions that, "dead" in themselves, are

liable to stifle thought; so, Bion advises, it is best to "stick close
to the fighting line" because "the further we get from it the more
ferocious the staff, the politicians . . . if they had their way the
bloodshed would be terrible" (Bion, 2005, p. 95). He escaped
himself from being Tank Commander of the British Society to
what he hoped would be the light and air of California, just as
Alice escapes from the "hard smooth straitjacket" of "love" when,
at the beginning of *The Dream*, all the vertices are "upturned": "Last
night [the vertices] weren't at all respectable; much more like
farts and gerks rushing up and down alimentary canals" (Bion,
1991, p. 4). The tumult is the effect of the dream stirring the psychoanalytic session, and it leads directly to the sense of invasion that
may or may not stimulate catastrophic (developmental) change.
The "fighting line" in a psychoanalytic situation may be dangerous,
but it is nonetheless a less hostile environment for the "growth-
stimulating objects" (1970, p. 129) than is the staff or committee
room, where the illusion of knowing how to manage the distur-
bance is maintained.[13]

Where is the fighting line? The beginning of any adventure,
including the psychoanalytic one, is—as Bion often stresses—a
capacity to get in touch with one's own ignorance, since without
this, the protagonist will not be open to "the experience of which
he is a witness". He will not be able to muster whatever powers
of observation he may have been endowed with. Observation is the
key to self-knowledge, for "the thing itself is altered by being
observed" (1991, p. 216), and the scientific–artistic investigation
itself "stimulates growth of the domain it investigates" (Bion, 1970,
p. 69). A single-vertex approach is not conducive to knowing ignorance:[14] hence the way Bion opens his ears to a host of characters
who—despite their education—are highly sensitized to one
another's ignorance, and who comprise between them a fairly
comprehensive experience of that state, while opening windows
out of it at the same time. Euclidean geometry, once an "aid to
insight" (says the Doctor), has, over the centuries, turned into a
restriction, a "liability". So:

> DOCTOR: Enter the fairy prince to release the sleeping beauty.
> P.A. [Psycho-Analyst]: Namely? I think you should introduce the
>         characters as they come on the stage. [Bion, 1991, p. 224]

Multiple vertices (characters) enter the stage to "release" (bring to light) the sleeping beauty, the shape of the future self, the new idea of psychoanalysis.[15] Starting with the invasion of English Farm, Bion rewrites "Arf Arfer's little history of England"; this is his personal adventure, full of surprises. "Hullo! what are you doing here?" says Myself to Rosemary, a character who is "obviously present"—that is, who evidently exists now, not in the past, and whose personality is strongly re-presented (p. 114). Through such characters, he sets in action the "purifying effect of austere criticism", which he believed was often smothered by the "mental rubbish" of "fantastic admiration" or "complacent hostility" (p. 308), whether from others or from within himself.

Bion frequently complained of being forced to make up in quantity—through sheer repetition—what he felt his words lacked in quality. In the *Memoir*, he allows all his internal voices their say, despite the fact that when they all speak at once it is "Bedlam". We must be prepared for a tonal barrage ranging from absurdity to revelation, vulgarity to sermonizing, cynicism to sentimentality, convoluted wordplay to poetic ambiguity, incoherent "somitic" ejaculation to formal soliloquy. Are these a collection of "ghastly puns" or "first steps in a new language"? (p. 465). Perhaps it depends, as Bion said of his analysis with Melanie Klein, on how the communication is received. Eventually, a goal of "disciplined debate" is agreed by the Group (p. 443), but if this is to be "real talk" as distinct from "talking about" (p. 477) it must retain its vital roots in this somatic orchestration—albeit at times a "strange hollow and confused noise" (to borrow Shakespeare's stage-direction in *The Tempest*, IV.i.: 139). By Book Three, Bion has formulated the object of his story as a description of the meeting of the pre-natal and post-natal personalities, whose aim is to write "a single book sired by 'us'" (Bion, 1991, p. 466) through a creative interpenetration across the caesura, represented in bodily terms by the diaphragm that comes into operation at birth. He recognizes that it would require a "drama of Shakespearean quality" to properly describe such a meeting (p. 551). But, he says, he has "a date to meet Fate"; the end of his life feels like a "rush" and he must present his *Memoir* of what he hopes will happen in the future: the rebirth of psychoanalysis itself, erupting from the smouldering ashes of a state of genuine ignorance, a spark at which others may warm their hands.

The *Memoir* is thus a reticular structure in which meaning can slip through established lines of thought, or be held in tension between a variety of vertices. It aims to model a "psychoanalytic zoo" filled with "beautiful and ugly creatures", a "stamping ground for wild asses" as well as space for their reverse perspective, the "great hunters" of psychoanalytic intuition (pp. 5, 239). Like the animal rattling the bars of its cage to an "established rhythm" in *Taming Wild Thoughts*,[16] the *Memoir* finds a music of its own. These "fascinating animals", like the one-man-band of Bion's stammerer,[17] produce a "pattern of sound . . . each with a personality, like a real person" (Bion, 1977, p. 18), each making use of the "phonation" of a character we know, or think we know, called Bion—or is it Ourselves? Let the bar-rattling music begin . . .

### The lowly glandular origins of thought

In heaven
Meanwhile, as Psyche-Soma fought their war
Of contraries, I arranged for us
A barrier of communication,
A diaphragm of common-sense, to remind
The new gaseous medium of its once
Watery existence.
[Williams, "Confessions", ll. 71–77]

"The nearest that the psycho-analytic couple comes to a 'fact'", says P.A., "is when one or the other has a feeling" (p. 536). A feel-ing indicates that the barrier between two contraries—such as love and hate, pre-natal and post-natal—has been penetrated; this results in what he punningly calls "common sense". Then, those two com-mensal entities have the opportunity to become either parasitic on one another, or symbiotic and growth-promoting. And, in Bion's theory of thinking, the entities which "underly all the examples" in the pattern of their confrontation are Psyche and Soma: they repre-sent the original War in Heaven,[18] and behind them lies the nature of the primitive origins of mind as it evolved from brain.

Towards the end of Book Three, P.A. speculates on the feeling origins of the post-natal Group's quest to discover their identity:

P.A.:     Ultimately I would hope to find out whether there was some physically recognizable as well as verbally recognizable underlying reality which we are investigating, not just a vast mare's nest of thinking about thinking about thinking, which same "thinking" did not exist but was a symptom of glandular activity.

ROLAND:   Does the adrenal gland start us thinking, or our thinking start the gland secreting?

ROBIN:    Why not so of other glands? [p. 512]

P.A. then admits that his phraseology indicates an unconscious hostility to the "lowly glandular origin" of genuine thought (of the type which is not just "thinking about thinking"), and concludes that "Hatred of our origins seems to be inseparable from any advance". The need to acknowledge the debt to "origins" is confirmed by Alice. Various voices have already formulated the problem:

SOMITE TWENTY-FOUR:   If I had known I would grow a soul I would have remained a foetus.

TWENTY-FIVE YEARS:   If I had known I had such an ugly somitic ancestor I would not have tried to cultivate a soul.

EIGHTEEN YEARS:   I don't think I knew your somitic friend, but I had my suspicions and thought a soul would be an asset, not an excrescence. [p. 461]

Even when the Group appear on the verge of achieving their "disciplined debate", they try not to lose sight of eruptions of denial regarding the origins of their thinking process in pre-natal life.

The story of Bion-as-group, therefore, begins with a "speculative" science-fiction about the nature of the pre-natal or proto-mind. An inadequate "language of experience and reason" has to be borrowed from post-natal existence to convey the drama of the somites (mind–body elements) which comprise the em-mature personality—"emmature" suggesting embryonic maturity (in process of becoming) rather than simply immaturity:

EM-MATURE:   My earliest experiences were of something touching what I later heard was "me". The changes in pressure in the fluid surrounding me varied from what Me called pleasure to what Me called pain. My optic and auditory

> pits at the age of three or four somites received sound
> and light, dark and silent, not usually increasing beyond
> nice and nasty, but sometimes making me feel more inan-
> imate than animate. [p. 430]

Em-mature, though he does not speak after "birth", is the hero of
the narrative, with roots in the somitic core of the personality, at the
foundation of dream-life. As P.A. says, "If somites could write, the
book would be 'On the Interpretation of Reality', and the theories
would all be what we call dreams" (p. 470). His ambition is to be
represented Shakespeareanly in "a tale told by an idiot" (p. 432;
*Macbeth* V.v.: 26). But Em-mature's search for self-expression is
constantly in danger of being pre-empted by the impatience of the
know-it-all aspects of the personality:

| | |
|---|---|
| PRE-MATURE: | Get on with it—when were you born? |
| EM: | Don't hurry; I was coming to that. |
| EIGHT YEARS: | You always are, but do not arrive. |
| EM: | When I was only three somites old—. . . [p. 430] |

When the first catastrophe of birth occurs, Emmature finds his identity split into the "warring twins" Psyche and Soma; it is the result
of his discovering (as Term) that his "mental membranes" enable
him to "reach far beyond [his] feet":

| | |
|---|---|
| MIND: | Call me Psyche—Psyche–Soma.[19] |
| BODY: | Soma–Psyche. |
| MIND: | We must be related. |
| BODY: | Never—not if I can help it. [p. 433] |

The introduction of Mind and Body to one another is contemporaneous with the biological fact of birth; and the confusion entailed
by the newly recognized distinction between sensuous and non-
sensuous is paralleled by the newly functioning diaphragm, which
marks the change from a watery to a gaseous medium through
which "meaning" seems not to penetrate, "whether it is from you
to me, or from me to you":

| | |
|---|---|
| SOMA: | If you had any respect for my "feelings" and did what I |
| | feel you, you wouldn't be in this mess. |

PSYCHE:  I am in this mess because I was squeezed into it. Who is responsible—your feelings or your ideas? All that has me is yours—amniotic fluid, light, smell, taste, noise, I'm wrapped up in it. Look out! I'm getting absorbed!

SOMA:  I'll pi you when I've absorbed you. All piss, shit and piety. You can idea-lize it—get a good price for it no doubt. Bless me—I'm getting absorbed too. Help!

PSYCHE:  That's what comes of penetrating in or out. I'm confused.

SOMA:  That's what comes of not penetrating—you break up or down.

BOY:  Let's leave them to it. [pp. 434–435]

The strange lights, noises, and turbulence within the womb, as Psyche and Soma separate from one another, recall the original struggle in the jungle—what Bion, in *The Long Week-End*, calls the "real night". They are "caught in a web of whirling waters" under the eye of Leonard (Leonardo), Krishna, and Milton with his "formless infinite" (p. 430).

This prototypal scene of hunting, penetrating, breakdown, absorption embodies the primitive origins of the artistic vertex. The dreamer goes beyond sensations of pleasure and pain to phantasies of projection and introjection, and thereafter is irrevocably locked in dialogue with an Other—a fundamental requirement for thinking, though Bion's point is that proto-conversations in the form of suckings and erections are already the basis of a thinking mentality or its reversal:

> Even the foetus develops a capacity for what is later called projective identification. In other words, it has feelings or primordial ideas that it tries to deal with by evacuating them—a primitive mechanism derived maybe from the physical capacity for evacuation, literally, so that the amniotic fluid is polluted with meconium. [Bion, 1997, p. 50]

The drama of linkages and evacuations was set in motion by the initial penetration of an ovum by a sperm "characteristically swimming against the current" (Bion, 1991, p. 429).[20] And amid the confusion is a hint that somehow, under pressure of the underlying Idea (the dominant life instinct), there may be other perspectives of "penetration" and "idea-lization" which could potentially relate "feel-ings" to "ideas", body to mind, on the basis of remembering their common origin.

The dialogue between Soul and Body is a traditional motif in poetry, and has always provided a basis for the kind of imaginative philosophical speculation about mental origins that Bion is interested in, and that (from his account) first struck him as a child when he noticed the animal musically rattling the bars of its cage. Marvell, for example, takes a standard religious formulation of the war between fleshly desire and spiritual morality and transforms it into a Bionic inquiry into the uncomfortable nature of knowledge and the problem of finding a suitable aesthetic shape to contain it:

> SOUL: I feel, that cannot feel, the pain . . .
> Constrained not only to endure
> Diseases, but, what's worse, the cure;
> And, ready oft the port to gain,
> Am shipwreck'd into health again.
> . . .
> BODY; [on the "maladies" of turbulent emotion]
> Which knowledge forces me to know,
> And memory will not forego;
> What but a soul could have the wit
> To build me up for sins so fit?
> So architects do square and hew
> Green trees that in the forest grew.
> [Marvell, "A dialogue between the soul and the body", ll. 24–30, 39–44]

The body is wracked by fear, love, hatred, joy, sorrow, "which knowledge forces me to know". Such knowledge makes it feel unnaturally architected, while correspondingly, the soul feels imprisoned by the bodily health that insists it "feel" when it "cannot feel", and in reaction, it wishes to escape its "bolts of bones" (Bion's exo-skeletonous mentality).

A more contemporary soul-and-body dialogue by Roland Harris pursues imaginative speculation about the soul's sensuous sheath into prenatal realms, as does Bion:

> Poor friend, for pity
> Ever to dwell
> With steel placenta,
> Meconium city;

Rusty placenta
Of steel dead
Long, so long after
Your dragon-deed.
[Harris, "Dialogue of soul and body", unpublished]

This dialogue is couched in terms of the mediaeval legend of Tristan (soul) and Iseult (body), whose tragedy is really that they are unable to trust one another, and "steel" refers to the "hard light" of the body's polished armour that never allows its inner "soft light" the reversed direction of birth, so the placenta rusts around its heap of soft meconium, long after the dragon-deed when the sperm penetrated the ovum. Later, Bion uses a similar metaphorical pattern in his story of the tank-like "cretaceous" skull, whose steeliness affords scant protection to the "alluvial" brains within it. "We must be related", said Bion's Mind; "Not if I can help it," the Body replies, suspicious of domination by this new invader.

The first image of potential creative communication is the diaphragm, which the post-natal Group imagine may become a "displaying screen" rather than an "obscuring screen", which might be used "as Picasso could use a plate of glass": as "a screen, a caesura, a resistant material between one particle and the next", presenting "meaningful pattern projected against the glass" (Bion, 1991, p. 465). The change from watery to gaseous medium is a reality that must be faced. As Term warns Em from the basis of pride in his new endo-skeleton: "If you borrow an exo-skeleton you will never get out of it" (p. 431). Em says, like Marvell's Soul bewailing its shipwreck into health, "I shall be so well and truly born I suppose I shall never recover" (p. 432).

In Bion's fable, the new endo-skeletonous mentality, based on the quarrel or communication of psyche and soma across the diaphragm, represents a catastrophic change from which there is no return. There is only one alternative to birth: the death of the idea, for as P.A. acknowledges:

P.A.: A foetal idea can kill itself or be killed and that is not a metaphor *only*. Metaphors can be the ghosts of ideas waiting to be born, and not only, as Berkeley said to Halley, "ghosts of departed quantities" [pp. 417–418]

As Bion puts it in *Taming Wild Thoughts*, "although we tend to have shifted our observations away from the body to the sphere of the mind, the body has not ceased to exist"; free associations do not mean that "the facts weren't facts" (1997, p. 44). In his view, the body-base of the mind, with its archaic "vestiges", is the key to our capacity to contain or symbolize meaning. During the course of *The Past Presented*, P.A.'s "impenetrable complacency" is severely dented by the continuous lynching of the other characters in the book; holes are made for the entry of understanding. His own "gas bag" jargon (as they call it) is in the process of becoming pregnant metaphor: not to be dismissed as "metaphor *only*", but metaphor as a body capable of containing the new idea, by virtue of the linking of vertices in some kind of aesthetic form—"science fiction".

### Running round the bend: minus LHK

By age nineteen, he said, his ways were set.
He joined the Tanks to penetrate the secret
Of their strength, and fired by intrusive
Curiosity, he watched on their home ground
The training manoeuvre as the tanks, slow
As saurians in some mating ritual,
Clawed each other heavily up the hill.
Playfully on sports day the small tanks
Tyrannosaurus and young Stegosaurus
Tossed between each them their communal
Rudimentary brain; but a permanent
Lodging for this anomaly within
Their armour plate was never found.
                [Williams, "Confessions", ll. 281–294]

In Bion's mythology of the human condition, the capacity to think is such a recent extension to the capabilities of the brain that the body as a whole is liable to reject it in a way analogous to foreign tissue. Can humans tolerate this unwelcome pregnancy-sickness? Before pursuing further the story of the evolution of the new Idea, I would like to put together a picture of the wrong alternative to being "born": the state of minus LHK—the escape from emotionality into a delusory self-preservation, whether this is body rejecting soul or soul rejecting body. "The impulse to inhibit is fundamentally envy of the growth-stimulating objects", as Bion put it in *Attention and Interpretation* (1970, p. 129). The shell of −LHK, which frequently takes the form of psychoanalytic jargon and single-vertex science, leads to "calcification" of the life-maintaining arteries. The exo-skeleton of obedience, arrogance, sanctimony, or respectability means that the idea cannot be born but dies *in situ*— as on the day of 8th August at Amiens, when Bion says he "died" but his body outlived his soul.

"What saurian engendered thought?" asks P.A. in *The Past Presented* (Bion, 1991, p. 352). Looking back to the previous book, *The Dream*, we remember the confrontation between the two dinosaurs, and the hostility engendered by their suspicion that a container for thoughts might be developing between them:

ADOLF:    What's that tiny little thing you've got up there?
ALBERT:   A rudimentary brain.
ADOLF:    Hmmm . . . I don't like it. Mark my words, it will burst your head open! Chacun à son goût. Ow! What's that? You've shoved your thoughts into me, you vile creature . . . If this fool Albert thinks I can't chew up his armour!
ALBERT:   If this fool Adolf thinks my armour can't wear down his teeth! [p. 84]

Instead of considering how to promote the development of mind from brain, they make a mutual attempt to eat one another. Bion calls this the battle of "Sade versus Masoch . . . Watch the Head Devour its Tale" (p. 119), because the dinosaurs fail to realize that eating and being eaten are in psychic reality merely parts of one reversible process: "Tyrannosaurus didn't like being eaten . . . what was amusing and satisfying was the same activity when the perspective was reversed and yet felt quite different—or so it thought. It was not different but 'reversed'". They are so busy arguing they do not realize they are "already extinct". It is an anti-aesthetic caricature of the transference–countertransference in which action has superseded thought.

And yet, says Bion, those "dead bones" have somehow "given birth to a mind" (p. 60). The "preservative function of the shell" postulated by Priest ( p. 478) has been completed. Much later, P.A. gets back in touch with his saurian sense of disgust at the monstrous birth of thought: "What an ugly monster it is . . . the product becomes capable of independent existence" (p. 352). The problem is not that the species has no mind, but that it does not know what to do with it. Roland explains the confusion in terms of aesthetics:

ROLAND  It is difficult to believe that the "mind"—shall we provisionally call it—has no boundary which is obviously and clearly bounded by the same boundaries as the anatomical brain. It is worse if it is seen to be inadequately represented by systems of analogues. Consider, for example, the struggles represented by the approach made to this difficult problem by the Greeks . . . [p. 78]

It is unclear where the mind's boundaries lie and in what way they fit into our picture of the human animal; we cannot comprehend it aesthetically. We seek for sensuous analogies, but they may be inadequate or false, as in the comic exchange with Tonks, the war artist (p. 155), that results in the image of the exploded tank:

O'CONNOR:  We burnt a fair treat. Some of us tried to get out, sir, and this made it look more real-like. The black guts pouring out of the hole of the "prehistoric monster"— just like the newspapers say, sir! [p. 156]

"Real-like" is a form of *trompe l'oeil* representation, a substitute reality to be contrasted with "thought" (p. 158), something correctly represented by Leonardo's elucidation of turbulence (p. 156). Rosemary, like O'Connor, is prompted to cut through Roland's circuitous philosophizing and reminds him again of her own beauty; she, who is an avatar of Helen of Troy, did not have to "go to school and learn Greek".

ROSEMARY:  I learned all I wanted to know and in less time than it takes for you and your lifetime of bellyaching noise. I learned, and Homer had the sense to make it possible for you to learn, that Helen was at Troy. One of you fools said it shortly and to the point— . . . "Anyhow, whore or no whore, she done it for him free", and that's what started all the trouble. [p. 78]

From an evolutionary perspective, the mind may be attached to the "nose or any other of the no-nonsense organs" (p. 60), giving another meaning to being led by the nose: nose-sense having its roots in the nasal caesura between liquid and fluid which harbours the thought-germ and generates tales told by an idiot, like Bottom in *A Midsummer Night's Dream*. Just as the brain hangs down into the nasal passages, so Bion suggests (following common parlance) that the sense of smell symbolizes the unknown receptor that, in contact with the mind's watery origins, can recognize the essence of a situation. "Falling back on a narrative view of the situation, smell can be one of the long-range methods of communication" (Bion, 2005a, p. 19).[21] Yet humanity is confused by an "asset" that is indistinguishable from an ass-like "excrescence" (as Eighteen Years complained). It "starts trouble", as Rosemary says. "Don't quarrel", says the Devil in *The Dawn of Oblivion*, politely offering his "nice chain reaction": "Tell me when you are ready and I will do what I can for you" (Bion, 1991, p. 463).

The result of failing to suffer the confusion entailed by thoughts being shoved into one's mind is pictured in the episode of the Cup Final at Wembley. The Cup Final recapitulates the Run of *The Long Week-End*, in which the young Bion rebelled against the intolerable "inchoate ambitions" aroused by the weight of the cultural past and exemplified by the classics scholar who was his primary rival in the long-distance school Run. Although Bion says that in his preferred sports he generally came very near to "playing the game for the sake of the game", the memorable instance of the Run was intended to demonstrate the opposite mental configuration: not so much retreat from aesthetic conflict as a terror-inspired reversal of it. It became associated later with the DSO, which he experienced as a scar of complicity in political mania rather than a badge of honour. He felt it to be a "sentence of certain death", both physically and mentally (1991, p. 149). Like the dinosaur, Bion felt he had to expel the thoughts being shoved into him by his alter-ego the classics-lover, and the emotionality they stirred. They could only be expelled by action—by running as if for his life. "Now the Mind . . . you just try it", says Alpha in the *Memoir*; "just attach it to your sensory perceptions!" (p. 60). It is Homo Sapiens' "new toy".

When the Mind is used for acting-out rather than for thinking, like a type of single-vertex science, it leads to catastrophe in the

sense of disaster. The final catastrophe of saurian man is prophesied
by Priest in his ecstatic sermon–soliloquy:

> PRIEST: Rudyard has ceased from Kipling. He has started his run to
> the wicket. From outside the main entrance . . . Here he
> comes and is just going round the bend! Look out! He's
> using an atomic bomb instead of a ball, and . . . I only am
> escaped alone to tell thee. What a marvellous day it is!
> Clear, silent, desolate. There is nothing to see but these
> gigantic boulders; I stand on top of one and look towards
> the horizon, a hard brilliant line that separates this brilliant
> desolation from utter blackness which is absolute—not so
> cold, so unfriendly as the googly . . . What's yet to come is
> still unsure. Man is a discarded experiment like the mam-
> mals, like the saurians, like fire, like sparks that fly up-
> ward, like troubles when there is no mind to experience
> them. [p. 398]

No container, he warns, has been found for the meaning; the meaning has not been suffered—that is, captured in aesthetic form and
thought through. Instead, the mind has been used as an atom-bomb
in a game of nuclear football—clever toolmaking man with his Big
Bang theory. This is the ultimate historical failure of symbol formation, equivalent to the date when Bion says he "died", his body
continuing to exist long after his soul had been extinguished by the
war: "The date in −K is August 7th and August 8th" (1918) (pp. 155,
257). It is "A-theist, A-chronous, A-moral, A-sthetic" (p. 159)—the
opposite of religious, scientific and aesthetic.[22]

The rigidification of the container into a false mental armour
that cannot expand aesthetically in response to the thoughts trying
to get in is imaged by the tanks of the War. Ostensibly scientific
constructions, they pervert the Tiger-god of Bion's childhood into a
type of vengeful pseudo-mother, who (in response to uncontainable
childish omnipotence) is driven to blow up or incinerate all the
internal babies rather than giving birth to them. This brings us to
the question of acknowledging the religious vertex, which is represented in its most sophisticated form by Priest, and obtrudes in its
most primitive form as "Arf Arfer", or as Alice's hallucinatory
Voice.[23] As with all three vertices—artistic, scientific, and religious—it is most vividly portrayed through parable, myth, or

dream. One such episode is the "otter hunt" of *The Long Week-End*, conveying a picture of the latency state (for which Bion also uses the story of Palinurus)[24] with its attempt to avoid all awareness of turbulence and to rationalize its fear of the Unknown, which, thereby, increases to a "nameless dread" through cat-astrophic splitting. The Otter Hunt is re-dreamed in the *Memoir* alongside aspects of the Tiger Hunt in order to demonstrate the reality of the Great Cat Ra.

### The Great Cat Ra

> That night Arf Arfer came
> In terror like the king of kings, the sun
> Obscured by the beating of his great black
> Wings. The hunt had killed a tiger,
> And to her mate the tigress roared
> Her requiem. Intense the light, and blackness
> Intense; as suddenly darkness fell and noise—
> Real noise—burst forth . . .
> The Great Cat Ra was armed to the teeth, no longer
> Content to passively absorb their sins
> With enigmatic smile. [Williams, "Confessions", ll. 119–131]

Out of the tameness of the pussy-cat springs "real night, real noise". As Tiger Tibs explains, the childish "devils . . . can't tell the difference between a flowerpot and a pregnant pot". These "golden boys and girls" sense uncomfortable stirrings of growth in their "silly boring old garden" (of Eden), yet the adult world reacts coyly to such stirrings and appears interested only in maintaining social proprieties (the "smooth surface of the Mediterranean", in the Palinurus story). The scene begins in Book Three with Tibs dozing in the sun, mirroring latency smoothness:

> TIBS:   It is nice to stretch in the sun. Not that there is much. When there is, that B'yrrh-Lady sends those damned children out into it. Why couldn't she keep them in her womb? Can't blame her if she chucks the devils out at *once* . . . The hell hounds always behave like a foetus—omnipotent, as old as God and as all-knowing, impossible to teach . . . "What a

pot!", the Boy said to his aunt. In fact it was the only scientific observation he had made, but his Mummy said it was rude. [Bion, 1991, p. 440]

The Boy's genuinely scientific observation is quashed and pseudo-science takes over with the smashing of the flowerpot by the croquet mallet as the Cat is released in a caricature of birth:

TIBS:  I am scared inside this pot I admit. I can't help running—all four of me. Stupid oafs! Woops! Up the tree and claws out. Lucky for them I didn't get my claws into *them* instead of the tree.

In this way, the children take revenge on their own first caesura, reinforcing their shaken omnipotence and proving "impossible to teach". The episode is interpreted by the interjections of a "Container" and P.A.:

P.A.:  They don't really hate each other—"they" all hate learning— it makes them develop—swell up.
CONTAINER:  It distends me. [p. 438]

The indignant Cat points out that "In the childhood of the race, at least the Egyptians respected animal containers for their content". But, as Moriarty had said in Book Two, "They think they are going to break down if there is a chance of hatching out" (p. 411). The Cat, in its ancient wisdom, recognizes that "The only time we understand and meet is digestion time and that language penetrates—in both directions—the barrier of sense; the sense that is born then is common" (p. 440). Digestion time across the gut, as across the diaphragm, symbolizes a genuine meeting of realities, a language of achievement which penetrates in both directions—a "common-sense" born from "a sense that is common" rather than the type that, as P.A. warns, "can resort to common arms" (p. 417).

As a result of the children's failure to digest the meaning of their latency mind-distension, the Cat prophesies a reversal of perspective: "Wait till the Great Cat Ra catches them in their dreams". Sure enough, when day becomes night, the hunter becomes hunted, as at the time of the Birthday Hunt when the Tiger's mate—his other self—returned to instil awe into the Boy's head-tent:

BOY:  Gd-ni . . . (sleeps) Tibs, you are a spoiled cat. No, it's no good
you saying you are a *Tiger*. If you are a tiger you are really a
spoiled tiger—a cat that has been spoiled and has turned into
a pussy cat. Cyril laughs when he says "pussy". He says it's a
gross word. Now don't you turn into a gross cat Tibs. That's
German. I hope I'm not getting afraid of an unspoiled great
Kat. Tiger . . . Tiger . . . we learnt in school . . . burning bright.
Please sir! Its eyes sir—what dread hands question mark and
what dread feet? A stop sir? Yes sir, a proper pause. If the wine
don't get you the women must. It rhymes with dust. [p. 441]

The degraded sexuality—the "gross pussy", the "spoiled tiger"—
opens, on the other side of the diaphragm of consciousness, into the
fearful, awe-ful, devouring ancient God. The Tiger's dread eyes,
feet, and hands are associated by the Boy with the power of women,
which is in turn inseparable from the fear of death (as in the recur-
rent nightmare of the nurse, for example p. 97); the military/school-
boy rapping commands already prophesy the "gross" fires of the
German army. The golden boys and girls fear that their growth—
their distension—will shatter their bright fabric into dust. The Boy
desperately tries to regain control by seizing the rules of grammar,
representing the rules of civilized society: "A stop sir?" We remember Bion's sister's comment in *The Long Week-End* when his electric
train came to a halt: "Full top?"—an episode which Bion compared
to his tank stopping years later (1982, p. 16); it is also part of Captain Bion's fevered dream under bombardment in the bunker (1991,
p. 54). We also remember his wry comments about how the use of
a compass, with its mechanical points of reference, is an "admirable
substitute" for not knowing where you are yourself (1982, p. 208).
But the punctuation with which he tries to control the power of the
image had been designed by the poet to project it more fully. In
spite of the "definitory caskets" of grammar and etiquette, the
rhythm of the poem—the underlying spirit of growth with its
inherent power—relentlessly breaks through to reveal the Sleeping
Beauty, whom Bion calls the Great Cat Ra.

Ra is the other side of "Arf", the uncanny laughter of "Our
father which art in heaven", the forerunner of catastrophic change
with its ambiguous potential. At the "faint sound" of arfing, Myself
senses the approach of his fundamental, generative dream and its
inevitability:

MYSELF:    My God! Here they come again. Those howls! It's eerie. I
           believe they are nearer. That! That! . . . That is a tiger. No:
           Tigers are only cats. That is no cat. Arf, arf, arfer's little
           history of England. You damned hyena! [p. 97]

For good or ill, the religious vertex—as distinct from institutionalized religion—has the power to shatter the Empire of Hypocrisy
owing to its ability to induce dream-transformations beyond the
control of the self:

BION:    Who, or what, is God?
MAN:     You do not know, but you behave and think as if some
         such force that is not you, "is". [p. 165]

### Strange meeting: Roland and Du

Just so, many
Incarnations ago, Satan slipped into
The Garden of Eden wrapped in rising mist, and
Inspired the serpent's head, possessing him
With act intelligential, abhorring not
My virgin's womb - no rib from Adam's frame
But an invisible blush on the white
Radiance of my eternity,
A noise inaudible, pain impalpable,
Not hell but hell with integrating force.
[Williams, "Confessions", ll. 79–88]

The not-you force that pierces the smooth surface of the latency
flower-pot mind and enables the germ of an idea to enter is imaged
by Bion in a little parable that takes the form of an encounter
between Roland and a pre-natal or somitic element of his personality named "Du". This "strange meeting" (Wilfred Owen) straddles
day and night, waking and dream thought. "The night, the dream,
is a 'roughness' between the smooth polished consciousness of
daylight; in that 'roughness' an idea might lodge" (Bion, 1991,
p. 268).

Du, an "awful looking specimen", is at first unrecognized by the
mind of which he forms a part.

ROLAND:  You're an ugly-looking devil. Who are you? Not the devil; a nightmare then? Not a nightmare? You aren't a fact.

DU:  I am the future of the Past; the shape of the thing-to-come.

ROLAND:  Not a ghost?

DU:  Do I grin like a ghost? How do you like these teeth? All my own. I fasten myself to your psyche—psyche-lodgment we call it. Most amusing.

ROLAND:  Get out you ugly devil!

Du (named after German "thou") is the intimate enemy within: the ugly, savage, Caliban-like foreigner who is, nonetheless, native to the mind's territory. He has teeth like the dinosaurs and grins like the Cheshire cat (which Bion associates with the power of "abstraction", p. 209), and compares his type of knowledge to that of a foetus: "Any foetus could tell you that". Indeed teeth are, like all excrescences, proto-thoughts. Roland's mind is defined as a kind of womb, and the question between him and Du is, how does an idea get out? What is Du do-ing with his "kicking around"?

ROLAND:  What the hell are you doing here Du?

DU:  I told you it wasn't hell—held perhaps. I can kick my way out of here easily.

P.A. speaks of "ideas [that] hold me whether I like it or not" (p. 257), and Du's place is "held" not "hell" (p. 275). He objects, in fact, to the rigidity of constraints liable to prevent his own birth into the world of thought; meanwhile, Roland is uncomfortably held by the idea he holds—"the shape of the thing-to-come":

DU:  I'm only an idea of yours. You abort me if you kick around like this.

ROLAND:  You've no right to be kicking around if you are only an idea—even an idea in the mind of God. Metaphors have no right to behave as if they were facts.

DU:  Words, words; words have no right to be definitory caskets preventing my birth. I have the right to exist without depending on a thinker thinking all day *and* night. Come inside.

ROLAND:  No thank you said the fly to the spider.

DU:     Said the foetus to the father—if I may use metaphors borrowed from the world for the living. An idea has as much right to blush unseen as any blush. [p. 276]

Roland is fearful of "going inside" in case he is trapped, like the fly by the spider, the tiger at Gwalior, or the boy in the tent of *The Long Week-End*. Yet all is reciprocal and ambiguous: who is hunting, eating, absorbing whom? Unlike the cannibal dinosaurs, however, Roland and Du push their dialogue through to the key problem of symbol formation and aesthetic form, in search of "metaphors borrowed from the world of the living". The usual discursive limits of language are inadequate; Du (like Hamlet, from whom he quotes, II.ii.: 192) objects to the misuse of "words, words, words" as a tank-like shell preventing the release of meaning.

The dream-dialogue between Roland and Du thus brings us back to the *Memoir*'s key concern with the relation between experience and aesthetic form: the problem of using words not as a protection against knowledge, but artistically, as containers capable of trapping a "roughness" beyond their smooth grammatical form, like the sculpture trapping light beyond its tangible sensuous form or like the rests in music (pp. 189–190). What is required is a marriage of art and science, elastic metaphor and hard facts of feeling—a stain on the white radiance/radients/radiants of eternity (Bion plays on all these variations). It is the stain that makes visible the suprasensuous idea beyond itself.

As the feelings—the foetal ideas—explosively surface, the chaotic, confusing Dream searches for a home and a transformation. So when Roland, stained by internal du-ings, asks, "Who'll buy my nightmares?", P.A. offers to take them on: "I will. If you have tears to shed, shed them now" (p. 282).

## The Party of Time Past

*Sir, you will write!* Yes, now he could write
Of his mother. Now he could give names to those
*Ante Agamemnona multi*, the unsung
Heroes and heroines of his inner life:
Kathleen who had the courage to become
The pregnant child with feral stare; Colman

Who showed him Ely riding in the clouds.
The pregnant *idée mère* that heralded
The loss of memory and desire. He sung
Of Auser and Roland the ones he loved, who braved
The hunter's shot of invading Man—the Man
Who believed in God's goodness, himself
An avatar of God, armed not with a toy
Electric train but with an automatic
Chocolate bar fuelled with lightning fire.
*Yes, that's his howl! calling his mate,*
Calling his partner for the becoming dance.
            [Williams, "Confessions", ll. 430–447]

The fearful prospect of a larger group meeting at which all the characters get together and confront their ghosts or lost, repressed aspects, with all the intolerable emotionality this entails, is in the air for some time before it takes place at the end of Book Two. "All change at Purgatory!" calls the guard at the Party of Time Past. The "transit camp" of the setting, though a "dismal hole", is an opportunity for change; this is accompanied by the music of the "resurrection blues" and the dance of "becoming" as the characters review their perspective on the story.

After Roland and Du, a whole series of strange meetings now take place on the lines of Wilfred Owen's "I am the enemy you killed, my friend" ("Strange Meeting"). Characters come face to face with parts of themselves that they imagined had been obliterated. The cloud drift is thick with Ghosts—the unsung heroes and heroines of Bion's inner life with whom he lost contact owing to prolonged "home leave" during the war—including those who (like Gates) "went sane before the war was over" (p. 423). In the general mounting anxiety, Roland is shot by Man, only to resume his place in the "disciplined debate" shortly afterwards: an indication that Roland–Robin–Man are rotating aspects of the same character. Man initiates the upturning of the vertices—something that is always ambiguous, since it is unclear whether he is a messenger from God or the devil, developmental or deathly—just as "shooting" is also a pun on growth spurt. Man points out that Roland's death (state of transition) was essential for him to become "available for my purposes", and P.A. objects: "Tom has buried him and he must be discomposed" (p. 394).

Dis-composure is, in fact, the key to catastrophic change in the purgatorial camp. P.A. sheds his "armour-plated mind", his "hero dress" uniform, and meets his ghost:

| | |
|---|---|
| P.A.: | I hardly recognised him—it's my ghost. |
| GHOST OF P.A: | I died at English Farm and I've been working through Purgatory since. I feared I might become like P.A. You only saw me wearing my Hero dress. I was afraid you'd see me—as I saw poor Gates. [p. 423] |

Gates was one of Bion's tank crew who had "shell shock"—which according to P.A., meant he "went sane long before the war was over". Bion sees the shell shock in metaphorical terms as losing the shell of self-deception and "going sane", coming into closer contact with truth and reality.

Whether the strange meeting takes the form of a long-lost ghost, or a part of the personality so split-off or inaccessible that it appears strange or monstrous, like a Caliban, these encounters materialize around the presence of a "feeling" that is demanding recognition. The Cup Final occurs in the middle of the Party and represents the negative vertex: escape from the feeling. The Dance that constitutes the Party's climax is the culmination of a sequence that begins with the image of Sweeting's thoracic wall blown off "exposing his heart". Sweeting (whose real name was Kitching; see Bion, 1985, p. 44)[25] was Bion's runner, positioned close by his side, and while dying he begged Bion to promise to write to his mother. The words "Sir, you will write to my mother" haunt Bion's consciousness thereafter. In terms of the present self-analytic reverie, Sweeting is Bion's sweetheart—the feeling part of himself who did not run for success as in his own school Run, but who linked him instead with the internal mother he could not bear to think about—since he knew that if he did so, his chances of survival were less than nil. The field dressing of glory and lies "could not render invisible his heart beating away his life" and became synonymous with all delusory exo-skeletons (1985, p. 44). The apparent callousness of Bion's unspoken reaction ("No, blast you!") is proportional to the depth of his pity, which he found unbearable.[26] Sweeting was his first baby, having transferred himself to the twenty-year-old Bion as mother in the absence of any other.

Perhaps it was at this point Bion adopted the "tiny vestigial spore of cruelty" that differentiates mind from brain (or computer) and grounds the psychoanalytic encounter in a different framework from either Sade–Masoch or David–Absalom, who are overwhelmed by the intense emotionality of the parent–child relationship:

> ROLAND:   You can't just have machines. There has to be some kind of vestigial brain to programme the computer. The tiny vestigial scrap of human cruelty . . . Where's Robin? "They" must have got him. Ah, the sea at last. The salt marshes and the pee-wees calling and the great clouds billowing past far above. Is the war over? From that warfare there is no release—no release. Daddy! Oh Daddy—stroke me, Daddy! [Bion 1991, p. 75]

And the internal Daddy replies, "Would God I had died for thee! . . . Oh my son Absalom! Past, present and future, all shrivelled up to a nothing—the heart of a computer!" Is Bion child, parent, or both? The only solution to the sorrow of Sweeting and all the other internal babies is to make something of that tiny vestigial scrap before the trouble flies upwards like sparks and disperses in the clouds of meaningless eternity. Cruelty is inextricable from developing a mind-brain to programme the computer; the internal object that enforces development is always experienced as having a cruel streak, as in the episode of the crawling baby-self in *All My Sins Remembered*. If this is embraced, not withdrawn from, it becomes apparent how it is also inextricable from the object that delivers sensuous love and nurture—"stroke me, Daddy!" At the heart of the beautiful life of the salt marshes (a metaphor for life itself) is the aesthetic conflict, the union of love, hate, and knowledge. That war is never over.

The strange meeting with Sweeting in the arena of "presented" (re-dreamed) memory represents the resurgence of "feminine intuition" into the computer-like, institutionalized dovecote. By this stage, Rosemary has emerged as Bion's heroine ("What a woman!" says Sherlock Holmes [p. 300]).[27] Rosemary has been well brought up by "the best of mothers", the whore who contrasts with the other one, "Mother England", who crucifies her sons. She is associated through her "hard animal stare" with the pregnant child of "feral eyes" (p. 24); with the fiery Kathleen of *The Long Week-End* (as also is Alice); with the enigmatic Mrs Rhodes and her hard-won knowledge of life and death; and, through her resilience (she has the serviceable soul/sole of a servant's boot [p. 424]), with the Ayah of Bion's childhood.

Rosemary's organ of control centres on obsession with her feet —her means of drawing attention to herself—just as (Bion points out) her mythological ancestor Helen is known to Homer only as a movement occurring on the walls of Troy, and her physical beauty is never described. She *is* that attention-drawing movement, a dance that stirs the air, like the sculpture that traps the light. Watching her feet is considered better observational training than using articulate speech (p. 143). As such, Rosemary becomes associated with the infrasensuous as well as the sensual—evidence of the "significance" of the kind of almost imperceptible movement that betrays the possibility of growth, awaiting the "revelatory instrument" of symbolic reception (p. 77). The "marriage" of Rosemary and Man/Roland (after his "shooting") is an offshoot of Roland's Shelleyan meditation on "the rosy hues of the stain on the white radiance of Eternity" (p. 85), later associated with "the blush on the walls of the uterus"; there is also a pun on rosy/Rosie (as she is called by Man at one point [p. 165]). Associated with these metaphors is the pun on feet–foetus (as in "feetal membranes" [p. 434]), which demarcates her only fear—the fear of childbirth— and is again associated with the "dread hands and dread feet" of the Tiger. This is the underlying reality that prevents messianic mania taking over during this episode.

"I let my mind make me up", announces Rosemary proudly, as she dismisses the use of eye-shadow, her metaphor for cosmetic forms of education (p. 407).[28] Then, to her surprise, she finds she is "danced off her feet" by Man, her equilibrium upturned, and confesses to "feeling awful"—a word which is always tinged with the sense "full of awe":

ROSEMARY:  I feel awful; I can't even faint.
MAN:       You have to be tough; you are dancing as well as ever. I felt upset when I first killed a man and saw how surprised he looked. He never realized he had been killed. Shooting isn't at all bad when you get used to the shock.

ROSEMARY:  It's a "shock" to dance with someone—as if you didn't realise you would be "danced with". I suppose P.A. would say it was "sexual". Priest would say it was religious, like Saint Paul being "converted" . . .
MAN:  Your feet are dancing all right.
ROSEMARY:  They are dancing *me;* I don't mean it to happen. Look at Alice—she doesn't mean it any more than I do. [p. 414]

"'I didn't mean it to happen'—the saddest words in the language", Bion said of Sweeting's death. But also, the most touch-ing: "stroke me, Daddy!", even though the apparent sentimentality may seem almost intolerable. "I died for you", says Roland to Alice, "but you thought I was being sentimental" (p. 464);[29] Alice could not stand being died for, any more than Rosemary can stand being danced with. Sadness—awareness of this gap—is the first step in knowledge. As Bion puts it elsewhere, "This sad event, this experience of sadness—where did it originate? . . . could it originate in the relationship between two people?" (Bion, 2005a, p. 64). The child Wilfred's emotional distance from his mother had been measured by her denial of sadness in the period leading up to his being sent away to school in England: "Moth-er! You aren't sad are you?" "Sad? Of course not!" as narrated in *The Long Week-End*. His parents also sadly confessed they had not experienced the "light surprises" of religious illumination.

Now, however, Bion's internal parents, in the form of the Corbett-like Man and the ayah-like skivvy who can weather any display of male outrage, are finally dancing together in the spirit of religious "conversion" and can share their experience of "shock"—the surrender of omnipotent control that results in catastrophic change and the sexual generation of ideas, the foetus-feet. Up until now, intolerable emotionality—sexual or other—has been associated with shell-shock or its pre-war equivalent in the sensitive teacher Colman with his reeling headaches, and with "inchoate ambitions" to do with personality development. Like Sweeting's heart pumping away its blood, the "gaping wound of my mind" is covered with an "ineffectual field dressing of lies". "You were always thumping", says Seventy-Five Years to Heart: "if not with fury, then with fear. Later it was love" (p. 452). Now, at the Party of Time Past, Rosemary takes the lead in shedding the coverings of cosmetics and field dressings in order to "let my mind make me up"—a new kind of shell-shock.

## Shell shock

Again the tanks purred on, then burst
Into flower and came to a stop, the black guts
Pouring out of the prehistoric monster,
*And this made it more real-like, we burnt a treat!*
Was that, he wondered, the transformation
Signalled to him lately by the intelligent
Fool? For though the soul shall die the body
Lives for ever. [Williams, "Confessions", ll. 350–357]

The problem arises when the "preservative function of the shell" is outgrown, yet the emotional intelligence inside cannot find a new mental make-up—a shape which is real, not "real-like". Shell shock is a measure of the difficulty that the human animal has in tolerating a mind being "grafted on to its existing equipment" (Bion, 1991, pp. 159–160, 168). Tyrannosaurus had complained that his tank-like armour plate made him a "sitting target" in the "invasion"; but on the other hand—as Stegosaurus pointed out—if he lets his thoughts get above themselves, "no wonder your head aches!" Thoughts that get above their rigid container are liable to expand their sensibilities of taste, sensation, and eroticism, and hence refine their possibilities of communication (p. 84). As Bion says in one of his Italian lectures:

When we secrete an idea, or when we produce a theory, we seem at the same time to lay down chalky material, we become calcified, the idea becomes calcified and then you have another impressive caesura which you can't break out of. An asset, a useful theory of conscious and unconscious, then becomes a liability; it becomes a caesura which we cannot penetrate. [Bion, 2005a, p. 11]

A concept which was once truth-ful becomes a type of lie, covering over a truth which was once known by somebody. It turns into single-vertex religion or morality and is liable to be used tyrannically. This process of calcification, says Bion, applies to "the whole body of psychoanalytic thinking". Such a body is represented by the dinosaur-like tank of the war.

The story of Bion's escape from the tank, narrated in *The Long Week-End*, is retold in the *Memoir* in the form of a dream. Thoughts get above themselves and shoot upwards from the hatch of the tank. The story becomes a parable of the relation between the "cretaceous" (rigid or chalky material forming a hard bony case) and the "alluvial" (soft and vulnerable brain-stuff). The first stage in creating an aesthetic symbol from the mess of the actual event consists in defining the biological–geological landscape of operation, and locating the "intelligence officer" within it. When a soldier has his brains shot out of the back of his head, Twenty calls them a "useless chunk":

> TWENTY YEARS:  I admired the icy cretaceous in front. If that sniper fires I hope it will be a good shot through the forehead and out at the back with the brains which are such a useless chunk ... I saw the mess bulge out ... "Where's your tank? You're no bloody use to me without it". [Bion, 1991, p. 454]

The soft soul-stuff emerges from the shell just as in prehistory the mammals superseded the dinosaurs of the cretaceous period, being a fitter vehicle for the newly functioning brain. The geological structure of the landscape at the "Front" (forehead), with its transition between alluvial and cretaceous, echoes this ancient ground for mind's origin. Thus, Twenty relates symbolically his Intelligence Officer's question:

> TWENTY YEARS:  When I came out of the Third Battle of Ypres and hardly knew whether I was alive or dreaming he asked me if I had noticed when the alluvial changed to the cretaceous. I couldn't even laugh. [p. 453]

On the commonsense level, the Intelligence Officer is an "intelligent fool", one of those whose imagination cannot stretch to the "fighting line" and who remains circumscribed by the map-table, just as Bion had described his reliance on compass-bearings as a substitute for knowing where he was in himself (1982, p. 208). Collusion with the mentality of the ship of fools in the staffroom behind the lines leads to "terrible bloodshed". But on the level of dream and metaphor, the various parts of Bion's mind are engaging with a different type of internal intelligence officer, to seek out the vital spark of wisdom hidden in the ashes of tank warfare.

It is gradually impinging that the cretaceous tank-shell is not a fool-proof protection against catastrophe when relied on unthinkingly. When used *instead* of brains it draws disaster, as the tanks draw the enemy observation-balloons massing overhead. Nonetheless, there is another sense in which the brains need to expand from their confines and intersect with O through mental sniper-fire, just as the Cat is released from its pregnant flower-pot so it can become a dream of deity. The seeds for this constructive catastrophic change are sown by the *present* dream of Twenty-One as he revisits the moment when he abandoned his tank during the battle of Happy Valley. The literal events of that day are recounted in *The Long Week-End*, but the story is told differently here: it is *dreamed*. Significantly, Twenty-One allows his story to be told by P.A. ("When I was Twenty-One . . ."), indicating the extent to which its meaning is being digested through the very act of narration. The post-natal Group have just agreed to form into a "small committee" and co-operate in recollection. This mutual transference puts the story on the road towards aesthetic form, "disciplined debate" as the post-natals call it:

P.A.:    I caught up with my leading tank. I knew the long-range naval guns must get us. "Get out!" I told them, "and walk behind till it gets hit". I set the controls at full speed and got out myself. It raced—for those days—ahead so we could hardly stumble up with it. And then—*then!*—the full horror came on me. Fool! What had I done? As I scrambled and tripped in my drunken influenza to catch up with the tank, in the shadow of which I had ordered my crew to remain sheltered, my ice-cold reality revealed a *fact*: The tank, in perfect order, with guns, ammunition and its 175 horse-power engines, was delivered into the hands of the enemy. Alone, I alone, had done this thing! My pyrexia left to rejoin its unknown origin.

PRIEST:    How did you get in—by beating your hands on the cold steel doors?

P.A.:    I was in; I did get in. A high-velocity shell struck; without thought I shot out of the hatch as the flames of petrol swathed the steel carcass. Are you hurt sir? No—fell on my arse. Are you all right sir? Of course! Why? Home—quick! [Bion, 1991, pp. 475–476]

On the literal level, as in *The Long Week-End*, the young officer under the influence of fog, flu, and alcohol has saved the lives of himself and his men from society's common-sense, common-arms madness: escaping not only from the German guns but from the British court martial (equally an enemy to life):

> P.A.:    I thought I would be court-martialled. I was surprised that I told such an articulate, coherent story that I couldn't detect a chink of falsehood in it . . . All lies and so completely factual . . . [p. 475]

On the dream-level, the Blakean image of the officer shooting out of the burning tank, baptized in flames, becomes—in the context of the book—a metaphor for the birth of thought, like Athene springing from the skull of Zeus. It was of course impossible for him to get back in the tank; but in metaphorical terms, the tank commander is torn out of his psychical shell beyond his conscious intentions, owing to contact with more primitive yet more finely tuned instincts from the somatic, somitic levels of his existence. The origin of his "p.u.o." (pyrexia of unknown origin) is, in fact, O. He suffers an "eruption of clarity", an "outbreak of sanity". Afraid of looking a "fool", he momentarily squeezes himself back into obedience-to-orders; but then finds his body and self overtaken by an alien force, a force he had forgotten lay inside him; meaning has penetrated the diaphragm. The image of his escape parallels yet reverses that of the brains shot out of the back of the head; his "hidden reserves of intelligence" have been "impressed", as they were when he observed the "sleepwalking" infantry who simply did not move while they watched the tanks "purring" on to their destruction. He has engaged with a different type of intelligence officer, a different type of sleepwalking through dreams.

## The birth of psychoanalysis

> And yet I sense
> How from the beauty of my ugliness
> May one day spring forth mind, a light
> Brighter than a thousand sons.
> [Williams, "Confessions", ll. 66–69]

Bion's young men stumbling along in the shadow of the tank do, in a sense, grow into his "small committee" of Post-natal Souls (founded in Book Three, *The Dawn of Oblivion*; p. 474). They are the ghosts who become his sons, his multi-faceted self; they help to shape the genre of the new art-science of psychoanalysis that Bion says is still in its "fumbling infancy" (1991, p. 130). The Group become increasingly aware of "the Future casting its shadow before"—which is, as Alice says, equivalent to "the Past casting its memory forward" (p. 469). The penumbra of the past and the penumbra of the future converge on a beam of darkness in the present. In the final movement of the *Memoir*, which focuses on the idea of death as the next caesura in the life-cycle of Em-mature, they use the shadow to shelter from extinction while they gather their wits. At the same time, they are learning to observe their own function as capable of registering this shadow in a form which has aesthetic coherence. When they are at the same time observer and observed, hunter and hunted, all the voices can be "awake" and present their distinctive vertices, not in confused medley, but in the context of "a fairly disciplined debate" (p. 443). It becomes imaginable that talk itself could have a "reality" as great as action, and hold emotional meaning:

> P.A.:  We do not know if this conversation is "just like" talk, a "prelude" to talk, the thing-in-itself, fact, real. It may be "It", what our lives have been leading up to. [p. 477]

This prelude is to the kind of talk that is called "psychoanalysis"; the shadow of the tank, rather than its shell, could become a container for dangerous meetings such as that of the pre-natal and the post-natal personalities (p. 551).

It has now become clearer in what sense an analytic session is "comparable with going into action", as Roland queried, to which P.A. replied: "Anyone who is not afraid when he is engaged on psycho-analysis is either not doing his job or is unfitted for it" (p. 517). It is as dangerous as all art forms that put different aspects or vertices of the mind in potentially explosive contact with one another. The pressure increases to define the usefulness of psychoanalysis—to present it as a viable Idea. It is probably "too late to stop a mind developing", says P.A. resignedly; "the only question is, how to make the best of it" (p. 474). If practising psychoanalysis is "making the best of a bad job", yet at the same time "it has always been the bad jobs, the hated jobs, that made some sense of me" (Bion, 1985, p. 61): that is, that organized his internal group in a more aesthetic pattern and made its ugliness beautiful. Could this method have a wider relevance?

The method enables the mind, or pair of minds, under scrutiny to negotiate the process of catastrophic change in the shadow of the future, gradually drawing a "contour map" of the contributory configurations and levels of consciousness (Bion, 1991, p. 470). The mind can discover what the body thinks and vice versa. What appears to be terminal breakdown or shell-shock might on closer inspection—as Roland suggests—be more ambiguously described as "Break up, down, in, out, or through?" (p. 539).

Yet is psychoanalysis to be "taken" in the way the courtiers swallowed their lethal dose of single-vertex religion at Ur? P.A. offers it to Alice:

> p.a.: Here—suck one of these psycho-analytic pills—slowly. Just let it dissolve in your mind. You've swallowed it! You shouldn't have done that. It won't do you any harm—just a bit of heart ache. But it will spread through your system and be excreted harmlessly by your mind . . . [p. 469]

The dependent basic-assumption style of psychoanalysis is unlikely to be durable; indeed, taking Ur as an example, it is likely to be ravaged by its opposite perspective, single-vertex science.[30] It is as inefficacious as a field-dressing. What is required is an aesthetic apparatus that holds different vertices in tension, under alignment with O the unknowable. Multiple vertices—not sequential but simultaneous—can hold more meaning: "The phenomena which I regard as conjoined and mental are more full of meaning if I conceive of them as contemporaneous" says Myself (p. 193). So when Roland asks, "Can't this be done without an apparatus which is so costly in time and money?", P.A. replies "No; mental pain requires careful handling" (p. 535).

Mankind, as we learned from the Cup Final, is at its most vulnerable with a mind that it does not know how to use; it is liable to become one of "Nature's discarded experiments" like the dinosaurs

(p. 398), or to disappear in a "puff of smoke" along with the "cloud-capp'd tow'rs" of its imaginative structures (p. 540). Gradually the committee realize that the best genre for receiving and containing potentially explosive "facts" is a form of "science fiction", despite some initial resistance: "But this is pure conjecture! Is there no scientific proof?" In spite of various attempts to resurrect "premature" explanations (anything that sounds "more reasonable", that conforms to Priest's definition of scientific truth as "truth modified to lie within man's comprehension"), their dependence on "science fiction" for survival is reluctantly acknowledged. Like all art forms, this is more "perspicuous" and "makes communication possible through the barrier" (p. 539). For the group mind has expanded from the restrictive shells of both single-vertex science and tyrannical superstition, and is learning to engage in "speculative imagination, speculative reason". This stimulates a post-natal awareness of the dormant pre-natal talent for "sense[ing] the imminence of an emotional upheaval" (p. 538). Concentration on the "pattern" which, like radio-receptors, they receive and recognize within themselves, gradually dominates the primitive fear of being "swallowed up" by alien ideas. They accept that humanity needs to develop the "germ of phantasy" from which both science and art originate.

This is the germ associated with the "blush on the walls of the uterus" which, like the rosy stain on eternity, indicates an environment in which a growth-point may take root. Bion's metaphors dissolve into one another in his attempt to indicate the possible nature of a "phenomene" of mental inheritance that might correspond to the biological laws of Mendelian inheritance, beginning always as a "figment" of imagination. As death–birth approaches, the Group have premonitions that if "post-Natal Souls get together . . . a mind will be generated", like "maggots in a rotting dung-heap", and this fills them with anxiety (p. 474). The emergence of ugly figments such as maggot or spirochaete is co-extensive with the principle of beauty–ugliness than has run through the ages, crystallizing into figures such as Helen, Rosemary, and Old Woman. "Could beauty help?" asked Rosemary in Book One, *The Dream* (p. 130). Now Alice, through her hard-won identification with Rosemary, is able to speculate further:

ALICE:  Helenex of Troy, Cleopatra, are more than mere shadows of
the past; they could be the shadow cast before by the Future
we do not know.

P.A.:  Out of the rotting syphilitic remains of human flesh—

ALICE:  How elegantly, how poetically, you express it!

P.A.  —may the warmth engendered by the decay give rise to a
new form of life. [p. 486]

Bion's implication is that, given artistic or fictional nurture, responsive to beauty–ugliness rather than to lies–morality, psychoanalysis
may itself become a "new form of life", not just (as Priest warns)
another fashionable religion to be followed and then "heard no
more" (p. 544).

In the "pattern underlying all the examples", therefore, true
aesthetic quality is to be found by "abandoning" oneself to the
psychoanalytic process, which requires focusing on the diaphragm
or caesura between contraries in such a way that alien or ugly
qualities can find their place in the pattern. The realignment is experienced as "feelings"—a word much devalued outside poetry,
but one whose meaning Bion continually tries to restore and again
make poetic, at least in the confined context of psychoanalysis.
From the pattern that collects at the caesura, on the basis of tensions
and interpenetrations, the new idea can emerge in the fledgeling
form of speculation. This leads to structural development of the
mind, something which is logical but not inevitable or automatic;
at the next phase, the caesura will become a receiving screen
for further feelings which nonetheless follow a similar pattern of
resolution.

In the beginning, Em-mature had exclaimed—"It is terrible to
dream I may become like Term one day. If only I could be sure to
be told by an idiot I would be reconciled to being *Nothing*, but—
. . . (p. 432). As his life-span "comes to Term" and he nears the end
of his "psycho-embryonic" book, the metaphor of life-after-death
becomes synonymous with the "independent existence" of thought
itself. The previous vehicle, like the tank, is "nothing" and its "tale"
(story, or endpoint) is everything. Roland satirically exposes the
complacency of P.A.'s definition of man's "final" state as one of
"ceasing to exist":

ROLAND:    Why "finally"? This conversation, carried on by the
indulgence of the very gas which has supported our existence may be a prelude to yet another transformation
into the gas we use and abuse. "Spirit" or "soul" we call
it. Grandiose to the last. Homo sapiens! [p. 527]

Roland's "bitterness" nevertheless results in his expressing a meaning beyond himself, and beyond P.A. whom he had called a "gas-
bag". The Group pause in silence as the implications of the
"harmless conceit" sink in. Their conversation is perhaps becoming
"It: what [their] lives have been leading up to". Spirit or soul seems
as monstrous to the Post-natals as does a baby to a foetus, or a
"rudimentary brain" to a dinosaur. The "foetal idea" is thus something that will be born from the getting-together of the various
vertices represented by members of the Group. It happens when
"our forgotten fishy, amphibian, terranean selves all meet in the
same body at the same time" (p. 501), and takes shape in a
metaphor as a "ghost waiting to be born".

Psychoanalysis itself is such an idea. It existed Platonically, in
Bion's view, as "an example of a thought which, before Freud
existed to think it, was 'without a thinker'" (p. 168). Like the
Sleeping Beauty, it awaited discovery by a mind or mental configuration suited to receive it. Yet when the question comes up, "who
created or owned the idea?", Priest answers by means of another
question: "who owned the owner—God or man?" (p. 561). It is not
*only* a metaphor to speak of the "life" of ideas, P.A. had said earlier
(p. 417). The idea has a life of its own, but is not necessarily available
for use without its "thinkers", who mediate the shadow of its future:

BION:    Fancy? Or fact? Just fancy, if there was something about
ideas which might make them "generative"! The transmis-
sion of ideas may not follow the biological laws of sex, or
the Mendelian laws of inheritance. Alice may fear ... the
movement of a "phenomene" in her mind. When an "idea"
is created there is, in addition to the actual creation, a series
of reactions to the created idea. [p. 572]

The "series of reactions"—a metaphor derived from nuclear fission
—includes us, his readers. Like a Joycean "idée mère" (p. 196), it
generates further processes of becoming.

The book is itself one of those diaphragms between minds that may or may not become a receiving screen like Picasso's sheet of glass. Potentially it is "polyvalent", arousing identifications in multiple directions.[31] As Shakespeare put it when Prospero broke his magic staff and handed steerage to the audience:

> Gentle breath of yours my sails
> Must fill, or else my project fails.

Literally, he is requesting applause; but like Bion, he does not want "fantastic admiration" any more than he wants "complacent hostility". He is asking for the breath of life to fill sail or caesura and awaken the sleeping beauty of the "real psychoanalysis" (Bion, 1997, p. 34). Bion's self-analytic dream has been a process of excavating this underlying, basic, fundamental reality. It carries the spark of sincerity at which others may warm their hands, becoming an "idée mère". For as Keats said in his description of the "vale of Soul-making": "There may be intelligences or sparks of the divinity in millions—but they are not Souls till they acquire identities, till each one is personally itself" (letter to G. and G. Keats, February–May 1819; Keats, 1970a, p. 250). Bion's personal legacy to humanity is to model the process that Keats calls "a palpable and personal scheme of redemption". Reciprocated by its readers, such a scheme can become a generative idea for "the growth of wisdom"—something for which there is "no substitute" (Bion, 1991, p. 576). Heaven lies not in arrival at the inn (the "song of the sirens"), but in the journey (Bion, 1985, p. 52).

Bion questions, in *All My Sins*, whether we are able to recognize the "minimum conditions necessary for the growth and nourishment of a population of sailors, airmen, poets"? (1985, p. 55). This is also the crucial focus of the post-natal Group's last discussion. It takes us right back to the beginning of the journey, to what Roland calls "downy ignorance" (1991, p. 573): to "I am, there fore I question" (1985, p. 52). P.A. replies to Roland: "Down serves the fledgeling; mental down preserves us, however praise- or blameworthy we may be". Out of downy ignorance, like beauty's rotting compost, a fresh vision can grow—provided we do not identify too exclusively with the shell of the personality.[32] So, "to come back to tomorrow's session: what you have to do is to give the germ of a thought a chance" (Bion, 2005, p. 13).

*And does the thing have independent existence?*
Too late, says the mocking bird, too late—
She's gone, remembering all your sins.
He was only a small stain on the red
Radiance of my eternity, the merest
Instant in the never-ending realms
Of our becoming. But since our dances,
Like the poets' phrases, cast their shadows forward
Beyond the knowledge of their generation,
We could view his story as a trap
For light, fusing with integrating force
Its web of contraries to generate
An underlying pattern, a container
For that ugly monster the kicking
Foetus of thought, product of his birth
And death—which are only, after all,
Directions of the same activity,
So next time it endeavours to take form
The ending may be a happy one.
[Williams, "Confessions", ll. 494–513]

## Notes

1. *The Four Quartets* are often seen as Eliot's spiritual autobiography. Bion disliked Eliot, in fact, for his sneering manner of writing about Milton (a type of envious rivalry).

2. See "'Underlying Pattern' in Bion's *Memoir of the Future*" (the first paper on the *Memoir* to be published: Williams, 1983a, reprinted in Mawson 2010), and "The Tiger and 'O'" (Williams, 1985).

3. For a variety of reasons, the film was never completed. The basis for the script was the chronological story of *The Long Week-End*, expanded and interleaved with dream-sequences from the *Memoir*.

4. "Confessions of an emmature superego: or, the Ayah's lament", in Williams (2005a, pp. 221–235).

5. See Rosemary's comment: "If anyone ever reads this book it will be because of what the reader has the cheek to call 'pornography'. That is why Bion mentions me and he can't even make the description plausible" (1991, p. 146).

6. As James Olney has suggested, autobiography, while having an "enfolding consciousness" that constitutes its own commentary on itself, also "requires the reader to continue the experience into their

own lives" (Olney, 1980, p. 26). Although it may seem contradictory to claim to be marrying an objective study of genre with a subjective response to the work, this is in fact what the most sophisticated philosophers of aesthetic criticism—from Coleridge onwards—have always maintained is not merely possible, but necessary. (I have written about this in Williams, 2010.)

7.  See Donald Meltzer's description of psychoanalysis as a search for "congruence of internal objects" (Meltzer, 1983, p. 46) or, as he also saw it, a "conversation" between internal objects.

8.  This and further verse quotations at the head of each section, with line references, are from "Confessions of an emmature superego", my versification of the story told in the unfinished film of the *Memoir* (see note 3 above). The verse narrative tells Bion's Dream from the viewpoint of the Ayah-as-goddess.

9.  Sherlock Holmes, adapting Hamlet's words to Horatio (I.v.: 174–175), says: "Broaden your ideas, Moriarty. More things are wrought by crime than are dreamt of in your morality" (p. 310). The pun suggested by the juxtaposition of the two words is borne out by the fact that Moriarty, as in Beerbohm's cartoon, is always well-dressed, in line with morality's impeccable covering of respectability. This is associated by Bion with "lies" (as in 1970, p. 117) or with religious "cant" (as in 1985, p. 43), as distinct from spiritual religion. The liar knows the truth but turns away or covers it over.

10. English Farm was also the name of a battleground in the First World War.

11. An adaptation of Browning's "cloud rift" of famous names, "so thick they are anonymous", quoted in Bion, 1991, p. 120.

12. Bion is probably also thinking of the dovecote allegory in Plato's *Theaetetus*, which is concerned with the active–passive nature of the memory-hunt.

13. Donald Meltzer would call this the claustrum of the "head-breast", the "delusion of clarity of insight" (see Meltzer, 1992).

14. Bion considers that the three vertices of science, art, and religion need to be held in a constructive tension (see, for example, Bion, 1973–1974, Vol. I, pp. 95–96). Any single vertex is liable to lead away from the truth; it needs to be re-aligned with O (the unknown) by remembering the other vertices.

15. The "sleeping beauty", in a metaphor frequently used by Bion in his late talks, is psychoanalysis lying asleep among thickets of jargon or dead wood (e.g., 1997, p. 37).

16. Bion describes how, as a child, he observed an animal at the zoo rattling the bars of its cage with a proper "established rhythm that could be written down", something confirmed by his accompanying "very perceptive grown-up" (1997, p. 31).

17. Stammering, he suggests, can indicate the presence of a "third" person in the psychoanalytic situation who is using one of the partners as a "mouthpiece" (Bion, 1991, p. 568). Bion regards this third detached, observing vertex as essential to the process (on "third" and further "objects", see also Bion, 2005b, p. 19).

18. The "war of contraries" refers to *Paradise Lost*, with its war in heaven and the "hateful siege of contraries" (love and hate) experienced by Satan when confronted with the beauty of the new world, which he has contrived to enter despite the angelic guard set by God.

19. Bion does not set much store by any apparently sophisticated distinctions between mind, soul, and psyche. In *Sins* he writes—"And now I was supposed to be part of the psychiatric service—dealing with the psyche. Not the soul exactly—that was the job of the Chaplain's Department—just the psyche if you know what I mean (because I don't)" (1985, p. 47).

20. In Meltzer's picture of prenatal life, the placenta is already experienced as the primary feeding object (Meltzer & Williams, 1988, pp. 43–44).

21. Gerard Manley Hopkins, one of Bion's favourite poets, has written of the connection between identity and smell or taste: "my selfbeing, my consciousness and feeling of my self, that taste of myself, of *I* and *me* alone and in all things which is more distinctive than the taste of ale or alum, more distinctive than the smell of walnut leaf or camphor" (Hopkins, 1953, p. 297).

22. Bion points out, however, that most people have experienced mental death, and the only requirement for this is to have experienced life (Bion, 1991, p. 178).

23. The Voice is also heard at times by other characters, but it is Alice who is held responsible for it.

24. See for example Bion, 2005a, pp. 101–102; 1985, p. 17. As he puts it in his *Tavistock Seminars:* "in these turmoils—like the period of adolescence in the individual—various features that have been latent or unobserved beforehand become apparent, sometimes negatively" (2005b, p. 71).

25. Note the replacement of the idea of "kitsch" (nostalgic, sentimental art) with true sweetness, and its link with the discomfort Bion often expresses about his own "sentimentality" (as he thought his feelings might appear, in the eyes of others).

26. Compare the "cruelty" of the episode with his infant daughter in the context of psychoanalytic faith (Bion, 1985, p. 70).

27. I discussed the genesis of Rosemary as Bion's Muse in "Rosemary's roots" (Williams, 2005b).

28. As in Bion's statement "our minds are made up for us by forces about which we know nothing" (1980, p. 69).

29. It is a developmental change from Roland"s "hard smooth coat of love which fitted like a straitjacket" (Bion, 1991, p. 12) which is the situation before the "invasion" of English Farm.

30. In *The Long Week-End*, Bion writes, "I felt that religion had not 'taken' even as effectually as medical inoculation (1982, p. 117).

31. As in Bion's description of a creative state of mind, "polyvalent" rather than "monovalent" (1977, p. 25).

32. In his *Brazilian Lectures*, Bion writes that when the "chicken" begins to hatch out, "the more the person is identified with the shell, the more they feel that something terrible is happening, because the shell is cracking up and they do not know the chicken" (Bion, 1973–1974, Vol. II, p. 15).

# CHAPTER THREE

# The growing germ of thought: the influence on Bion of Milton and the Romantic poets

"Or will they decay and die leaving only a shell, as the accepted rules for a poem might stifle rather than protect the growing germ of thought?"

(Bion, 1985, p. 55)

The above quotation from *All My Sins Remembered*, comes in the context of Bion considering what are the "minimum conditions" for nourishing "sailors, airmen, poets". Unreal protagonists leave their "shell" into which others may project their own self-importance.[1] But in so far as heroism in either mental or physical activity is real, it will leave a "growing germ of thought" after the bodily shell is cast, rather than vice versa. This is the test of a genuine "service man", poet or otherwise. Bion hoped that such qualities could also reside in the psychoanalyst.

In the *Memoir*, describing the feeling of how "light began to dawn" in his own mind, Bion lists along with Milton, Virgil, and Melanie Klein, some of his schoolteachers—"men who ought to have been famous" (1991, p. 560). For, as he says elsewhere (and often repeats),

[Many brave hearts lived before Agamemnon, but they drove to that long night unhonoured and unsung for lack of a sacred poet][2] ... I have no complaints about the complacency which is engendered by a feeling of success about achieving a psychoanalytic insight, but it is a great pity if it becomes ossified or fibrosed into a kind of impenetrable diaphragm which separates us for ever from our ancestors. If Horace could acknowledge the existence of poets long before him, I don't think there is any harm in our also acknowledging the existence of our predecessors even though they were never heard of. [Bion, 2005a, p. 23]

The present chapter is about some of those ancestors to whom it is possible to attach a "label", as Bion says of one of the stray or "wild thoughts" that came to him through Shakespeare, in the form of the apparently commonplace rhyme "Golden lads and girls all must / Like chimney-sweepers, come to dust" (Bion 1997, pp. 27, 32).

Bion was a poetry-reader from his youth. Among those who were lifelong influences he names Milton, Virgil, Homer, Shelley, Keats, Hopkins, Herbert, Donne, and Shakespeare, whom he called "the greatest man who ever lived" (1991, p. 432). Poetry was not always at the forefront of Bion's theorizing, but it certainly always lay behind it, and in his later years he made a special effort to clarify just why he thought poetry was important—for psychoanalysis, perhaps more important than any other epistemology. In an introduction to a projected anthology of poetry for psychoanalysts, he wrote:

> I resort to the poets because they seem to me to say something in a way which is beyond my powers and yet to be in a way which I myself would choose *if* I had the capacity. The unconscious—for want of a better word—seems to me to show the way "down to descend"; its realms have an awe-inspiring quality. [1985, p. 241].[3]

Bion admired the poets not simply for their beauty of expression but because through that sensuous "way beyond my powers" they achieved a meaning beyond themselves, founded on a special contact with unconscious thought processes. Echoing Shelley's declaration in his *Apology for Poetry* that "poets are the unacknowledged legislators of the world", Bion asserted the value of the "fresh fiery brilliance of truth the 'generators' did not know because it hadn't happened—when they wrote it" (1991, p. 234).

I would like here to briefly survey the influence on Bion's thinking of the Romantic poets, whom he termed "the first psychoanalysts" (*ibid.*, p. 385), and of Milton, their spiritual if ambivalent progenitor. Milton is quoted by Bion perhaps more frequently than any poet, especially for the passage in *Paradise Lost* in which Milton tries to come to terms with his blindness and asks the Heavenly Muse to transform it into insight: "that I may see and tell / Of things invisible to mortal sight" (Milton, III: 54–55). Bion often compares this to Freud's citation from Charcot about the need to "artificially blind oneself" in order to observe the inner world of self or patient. Like Milton, he identified with the artist–scientist Galileo, for whom the darkness of the night sky became a mirror of the dark night of the soul.

This employment of a mental telescopic vision is associated with a capacity to tolerate the loneliness that results from a sense of exclusion from everyday vision—the sort of loneliness which Bion says prevails when the analyst achieves a necessary "detachment" from his primitive feelings or instincts (1963, p. 16). Establishing a pathway for the future psychoanalyst (1970, p. 88), Milton ventured into the "void and formless infinite" without disguising his fears (*Paradise Lost*, III: 13), making a "serious attempt" to formulate God or ultimate reality (Bion, 1973, p. 36). He was "qualified by temperament and aesthetic skill" to be a good liar, says the devilish Moriarty in the *Memoir* (1991, p. 353), but "unfortunately squandered his powers by hailing holy light". Morality (from *mores*) is equivalent to what Milton calls the protection of "custom and awe",[4] something that hardens into orthodoxy and moralizing, which Bion sees as a form of lying. Despite the resulting "logical confusion" (as Bion put it) and the temptation to Moriarty-moralism, Milton clung to his internal muse and followed her "dictates" (*Paradise Lost*, IX: 23).

Lonely—"yet not alone", as Milton says; for the Heavenly Muse "visits [his] slumbers nightly" and, in words given to Eve the "mother of mankind", "God is also in sleep, and dreams advise" (*Paradise Lost*, XII: 611). Feminine intuition—Milton suspected—makes contact with the truth more spontaneously than masculine reason, and is closer to the "intuitive" discourse the angels use amongst themselves than is the didactic instruction which Adam receives from Michael or Raphael. As Bion expresses it, we are dealing with a "slow lumbering conscious" trying to keep up with a "flexible speedy unconscious" (1977, p. 25). Real loneliness, he said, occurs when the psychoanalyst becomes "detached" from his primitive feelings, the source of mental sustenance (1963, p. 16). In *Paradise Lost*, Milton abandoned reliance on the "custom and awe" of Christian doctrine in favour of pursuing "things invisible", despite the fact that this entailed an "obscure sojourn in the realms of darkness" (III: 15). Bion admired Milton's commitment to unconscious intuition to help him work his way out of depression (1991, p. 663). He picks up Milton's metaphor in *Lycidas* of the underground river Alpheus that periodically surfaces and that creates turbulence as noumenon pushes against phenomenon (Bion, 1973–1974, Vol. I, p. 41). This turbulence can only be weathered if an ability can be developed to refrain from action, for as Milton says in his "Sonnet on his blindness", "They also serve who only stand and wait". This (together with Keats's "negative capability") underlies Bion's definition of suffering-as-patience (1970, p. 124) and his distinction between the complex mentality of suffering and simple, single-vertex "pain". It is the strenuous poetic mentality, requiring a commitment and dedication of which Milton complained bitterly when he wrote that through poetry a man is "cut off from all action and makes himself the most helpless creature in the world" (1972, p. 7). For, as Bion frequently reminds us, helplessness and omnipotence cannot be understood separately, but only as a continuum.

Contributing to the analyst–poet's difficulties in this vulnerable state is the internal gang of basic assumptions that offer him an escape from his loneliness, or alternatively, imprison him in claustrophobia: "Myself my sepulchre, a moving grave" as Milton's Samson expresses it (*Samson Agonistes*, l. 102), "a cornered rat" as Bion puts it (1982, p. 262). Bion's hope for a "disciplined debate" in the *Memoir* that will take over from the "Bedlam" of his internal voices all speaking at once has roots in Milton's devils' parliament in Pandemonium.[5] The "clamour of psychoanalytic gang warfare", as Bion describes it (1997, p. 23) identifies not just a social but an internal problem, on the lines of Milton's description of the "savage clamour" of the "wild rout" that tore Orpheus to pieces—"nor could the Muse / Defend her son" (*Paradise Lost*, VII: 36). There is another vertex on this Christ-like sacrifice in Milton's last drama, *Samson Agonistes*, where the hero undergoes a catastrophic change on the strength of "intimate impulse" (l. 224), demonstrating Bion's conclusion in the *Memoir* that metaphorically speaking, "birth and death are the same activity" (1991, p. 352). Hence also, Bion took the title for the second volume of the *Memoir*—*The Past Presented*—from "present/Times past" in *Samson*, indicating the way in which memory revises and relives earlier "caesuras".

Together with emergence from "the void" comes Milton's pioneering exploration of symbol formation and its origins. Bion's "fishy primordial origins of mind" (1977, p. 38) have an earlier representation in the travels of Satan as he wades and wings his way across the "abyss" of Chaos. The "palpable obscure" of Milton's mental landscape, complete with black holes and air pockets, is mapped in relation to both the boundless ("th'extreme") and to new boundaries (Satan "gains the edge"). Transcending both masochism and fatalism, the satanic explorer becomes a type of Oedipus (as Bion first named "Inquiry" in his Grid) and learns a new kind of language that involves the transformation of somatic states. God teaches Adam to dream, but Eve is taught to dream by Satan. It is the prospect of Eve that inspires the serpent's "brutal sense . . . with act intelligential" and enables him to speak "with vocal tongue organic". As Bion discovered through his work with stammerers, contact with the "lowly glandular origins of thought" may develop into "a language that penetrates" and gives a new meaning to "common sense" (1991, p. 440). It is developed in Milton's picture through the serpentine undulations of projection and introjection. Essentially Milton tells the story of how, through Satan, a "germ of thought" (Bion, 1985, p. 55) implants itself in Eve's mind. Through this, mankind discovered the "paradise within" (*Paradise Lost*, XII: 587) and the way to "thoughts that are generative" (Bion, 1991, p. 572). Milton and Bion regarded poetry/analysis as a road to mental "survival" (Bion).[6]

Milton's Satan was the original embodiment of the "hateful siege of contraries", the experience of love and hate simultaneously (*Paradise Lost*, IX: 121–122). This was then adopted by Blake in his *Marriage of Heaven and Hell*, to become the foundation for his personal revision of accepted theology: "Without contraries is no progression. Attraction and Repulsion, Reason and Energy, Love and Hate, are necessary to Human Existence" (Blake, 1966, p. 149). The "contraries" are passionate but conflicting emotions that underpin psychic reality. Milton conceived Satan's fall as derived not from pride (as was traditional), but from envy—misunderstanding the nature of its counterpart, gratitude. Later Satan comes to realize that

> a grateful mind
> By owing owes not, but still pays, at once
> Indebted and discharged. [*Paradise Lost*, IV: 55–57]

He could not "suffer" his gratitude/pleasure (as Bion would say) and therefore became prey to his envy/pain, a single-vertex emotion. Once the envy–gratitude value system has been clarified in this epic journey, its implications are pursued through the "siege of contraries" aroused by the beauty of man and his world—God's "second thoughts" (IX: 101). Satan views Man "with wonder"; he "could love" this new baby were it not for the intolerable inner conflict aroused. This complexity of response is what Blake homes in upon, perceiving the heroism of the struggle. Following the same pattern, Bion expands Melanie Klein's theory of Envy and Gratitude (which itself refined Freud's pain–pleasure principle) into the Blakeian formula of Love, Hate, and Knowledge, thus preparing psychoanalytic theory for the explicit formulation of Aesthetic Conflict. Second thoughts indeed—as Bion acknowledges punningly with the title of his 1967 volume.

Like Bion with his Grid, Blake felt driven to "create a System". He saw this world of truthful imagination as being achieved through stepwise stages, which he termed two-, three-, and four-fold vision. In antithesis to this neo-Platonic ladder of insight was a state he called "Ulro" (Error). This was not a place of unpleasant emotionality such as hatred or envy, but rather, one of "non-entity"—a state of self-imprisonment bounded by meaningless sense-impressions. Bion likewise envisages, in contrast to the positive steps of the Grid, a "domain of the non-existent" that houses "no-emotions" (1970, p. 20), and whose no-meaning rebounds in the form of hallucinations or beta-screen.[7] The state of Ulro might appear rational and orderly but is in fact "not organized", since it is merely a rigid container that stifles intellectual inquiry. It is inhabited by those who have "no passions of their own because no intellect": just as Bion describes a state in which the links or relations might appear logical, but if they are not informed by emotion, they are inevitably "false logic" (1967, p. 109). During the War he clung to compass bearings, he said, because he had "no idea where he was himself" (1982, p. 208)—a state of substitute reality, ineffectually covering his mental disorientation, that Blake emblematized in his famous colour print of Newton (reason) measuring the earth with his compass.

Bion said he was not interested in a "*trompe l'oeil* representation of Paradise", and that the nearest he could get to formulating "O" (God, ultimate reality) was "passionate love" (1991, p. 183). Blake said his task was to "open the immortal eyes of man / Inwards into the world of thought" (*Jerusalem*, plate 5), and that this was achievable only by "looking through" sensuous reality: "I question not my corporeal or vegetative eye any more than I would question a window concerning a sight. I look through it and not with it" (*A Vision of the Last Judgement*; 1966, p. 617). He could see "a world in a grain of sand", and this was where the underlying reality that was God resided: "I saw no God nor heard any in a finite organical perception, but my senses discovered the infinite in everything" (*The Marriage of Heaven and Hell*, plates 12–13). Analogously, Bion searches for "intuition" as a psychoanalytic parallel to the physician's use of sense-experience (1970, p. 7).

Common to both Blake and Bion is the view that the lie-in-the-soul is not a complex structure of its own (like Milton's Pandemonium for example) but rather, an "excrementitious covering" of projections of the selfhood which needs to be stripped or melted away in order to reveal the reality that lies beneath: the "lineaments of Man", or in its "divine" form, Jerusalem—the mind of man delineated in its naked glory. The lie is an invention bound up with moralism and the omnipotent selfhood, and is mobilized against the turmoil of catastrophic change (Bion, 1970, p. 99). It ignores the omnipotence–helplessness of the infant (Bion), the fact that "we on earth do nothing of ourselves—everything is conducted by spirits, no less than digestion or sleep" (wrote Blake, foreshadowing Bion's alimentary model of learning, as also did Milton).[8] The omnipotent delusion of control (such as that involved in moralizing) is one in which "self-righteousnesses conglomerate against the Divine Vision" (Blake, *Jerusalem*, plate 13). Such lies affect symbol formation. Bion speaks of the "agglomeration" of protomental "elements" (beta-elements) as opposed to their "articulation" (through alpha-elements) into symbols which can be used for dreaming and thinking (1963, p. 41). The beta-covered selfhood is not just unaesthetic, but unthinking. It disguises the living "line of the Almighty" as Blake called it ("A Descriptive Catalogue"; 1966, p. 585).

Perhaps Bion's most intimate identification with Blake occurs through his use of the Tiger symbol. In Blake's famous poem "The Tiger", vision is refined through an onward progression of musical hammer-strokes:

> And when thy heart began to beat,
> What dread hand? And what dread feet?

It culminates in the "fearful symmetry" of the awe-inspiring union of contraries: "Did he who made the Lamb make thee?" In Bion's *Memoir*, there is an account of a children's "tiger hunt" in which the persecuted cat takes its revenge in the form of a night-time dream, metamorphosing into the Great Cat Ra with the characteristics of Blake's "Tiger": "Tiger . . . tiger . . . we learned in school—burning bright. Please sir! Its eyes sir—what dread hands question mark and what dread feet? . . . (Bion, 1991, p. 441). As one of Bion's characters says to his "Heart" a short while afterwards, "You were always thumping. Rabbits thump . . . it tells you nothing" (p. 452). But now, as the relentless rhythm of the poem gets into him (along with the rules of grammar) the beats become meaningful. The "agglomerations" of the boy's phantasy game give way to the "articulation" of the Tiger-god symbol, seen face to face; his self-righteousness cannot conglomerate against the Divine Vision. Released from his omnipotence, his mind can be remade in what Blake calls "the furnaces of affliction", where "indefinites" are pounded into "organized particulars" (*Jerusalem*, plate 55)—the "little children" of the inner world—just as in Bion's system the alpha-elements are winnowed away from the mass of beta-elements.

"Mental growth is catastrophic and timeless", says Bion; it entails "death to the existing state of mind" (1970, pp. 108, 79). In this sense, fear is necessary: it ushers in awe (Bion, 1991, p. 382), which stimulates Inquiry. Blake stressed that mental growth takes place in minute, undetectable stages, regular but not smooth. It proceeds in hammer-strokes or pulsations. In his poem *Milton*, the "daughters of Beulah" (the muses) stand by sleepers and feed their minds "with maternal care", and each of their movements corresponds to "less than the pulsation of an artery . . . For in this period the poet's work is done" (plate 29). The poet's work—and the analyst's too, as he or she "dreams the session" (as Bion always adjures his listeners). Through such infinitesimal disjunctions, catastrophic change is absorbed.

The analyst, says Bion, has to try to "become infinite" in himself, to absorb these minute shocks. He quotes Coleridge being pursued by an ambiguous "frightful fiend":

> Like one that on a lonesome road
> Doth walk in fear and dread;
> And having once turned round walks on,
> And turns no more his head;
> Because he knows a frightful fiend
> Doth close behind him tread.
> [Coleridge, *The Ancient Mariner*, ll. 446–451][9]

The road is lonesome, but the walker is not alone when in touch with his primitive feelings or dreams—"plumbing the metaphysic depths", as Coleridge described his philosophical pursuits. Bion's reference to Milton's river Alpheus is also to Coleridge's "sacred river Alph" in *Kubla Khan*, and indeed Coleridge specialized in ways of defining the strata of consciousness. These are the "caverns measureless to man", far beyond the reach of compass bearings, associated with O the unknowable, since man is the measure of all things that he knows (a dictum to which Bion also refers). Bion was perhaps more haunted by Coleridge's music than by his prose—in particular the military march of the "frightful fiend"; yet the most explicit proto-psychoanalytical formulations are to be found in Coleridge's metaphysics. These include: the language of projection–introjection, subjective–objective, and observer–observed, as in Coleridge's description of Shakespeare as one who "projected his mind out of his particular being [by means of] that sublime faculty by which a great mind becomes that which it meditates on" (1808; 1960, Vol. I, p. 188). Coleridge's distinction between mechanic and organic forms, or Fancy *vs.* Imagination, prefigures Bion's of beta-elements *vs.* alpha-function, or "agglomeration" *vs.* "articulation". Coleridge insisted on the need to make "the relations of things" rather than just things themselves the focus of inquiry, as did Bion with his theory of links. Like Bion and every true philosopher, he affirmed the Socratean dictum that "ignorance [is] the condition of our ever-increasing Knowledge", the point from which all the journeys start (Coleridge, 1957, Vol. 3, n. 3825). As with Blake, every idea "partakes of Infinity" and moreover, says Coleridge, "contains an endless power of semination" (1972, p. 24), as with Bion's "idées mères, thought generators" (1991, p. 196) - implying that in a sense *all* ideas are "idées mères".

The detectable influence on Bion of the Wordsworthian Idea is very different in quality—almost amorphous, fluid. Bion quotes the famous Wordsworthian principle of "recollection in tranquillity" (1992, p. 285) but with the opposite stress: on the need to "abandon" oneself to poetic immersion in the moment. This is the aspect of Wordsworth's poetry that permeates Bion's thinking, not (unlike Coleridge) his distinctions and clarifications. We might compare, for example, Wordsworth's account of skating in his childhood with Bion's spinning around under the hot Indian sun playing trains: "the devil had entered into me" (1982, pp. 29–30):

> Still the solitary cliffs
> Wheeled by me, even as if the earth had rolled
> With visible motion her diurnal round.
> [*The Prelude*, I: 458–460]

In each case, the memory becomes one of those mind-building "spots of time" (Wordsworth), to be associated with "that beauty which hath terror in it" (*The Prelude*, XIII: 225), like the child Bion's awe during the Tiger Hunt. Such generating symbols bring

> Visitings
> Of awful promise, when the light of sense
> Goes out in flashes that have shown to us
> The invisible world . . .
> Tumult and peace, the darkness and the light
> Were all like workings of one mind . . . [VI: 533–568]

As Coleridge described his experience on first hearing Wordsworth recite *The Prelude* to him: "The tumult rose and ceased" ("To William Wordsworth"). The "terror" of parental disapproval (in Bion's case) is converted into the "awe" that brings the experience to life—with "awful promise", remaining in touch with "the primordial origin of mind" (Bion, 1991, p. 648). "Many fear the awe-ful experience" (p. 382). Like his parents' sadness at their feeling of lack of "light surprises" (religious inspiration), such spots of time sing the "still sad music of humanity" (quoted in 2005a, p. 74) on which future development may be founded if it is not enshrined in resignation.

In the Wordsworthian vision, these vertical shafts of light, awe, or tumult penetrate a mystical blue calm much as in Bion's favourite metaphor of the stick creating turbulence in smooth water. The contrasts come together to represent the "workings of one mind". They are the generative ground of proto-thoughts, fished from Plato's lake, "moving about in words not realised" (Wordsworth's "Immortality Ode"). The banks of the Jamuna and the banks of the Duddon, whose murmurs "blend[ed] with [the] nurse's song" (*The Prelude*, I: 271) shared an imaginative identity. Both "drank the visionary power" from their childhood's land-scape, which spoke to each "the ghostly language of the ancient earth" (*The Prelude*, II: 328). This sense of envelopment followed them to foreign fields, as in Wordsworth's description of walking along the "level fields" at Cambridge "With heaven's blue concave reared above my head" (*The Prelude*, III: 100), or Bion's beloved Norfolk "blue skies and blue water" (1991, pp. 279–280), the blue-ness of its ether pierced by diving snipe (Bion) or by "awful visit-ings" come to disturb the "tranquil soul" (Wordsworth). In the "Immortality Ode", Wordsworth moreover identified the sense of loss or separation from the world of Platonic realizations ("child-hood"), which he explained as "custom" but which Bion then analysed as domination by basic assumption groupings.

If Wordsworth ultimately withdrew from the "terror of infinite space" (Pascal, often quoted by Bion, e.g., 1965, p. 171), Shelley revelled in its mystical potentiality, and like Milton battled with its plaguing presences. Shelley's universe of ideas comprises dazzling light, streams of particles, atoms, fragments of cosmic dust, waves, and cloud mass—all vehicles for, or obstructions of, meaning. Life itself "stains the white radiance of eternity" (*Adonais*, l. 463), a phrase often quoted by Bion, though he changes it to "rosy stain" (1991, pp. 51, 465)—for "an idea has as much right to blush unseen as any blush" (p. 276).

Bion in *Transformations* notes Shelley's interest in how the force of sensations can confuse thought with its objects; he quotes Shelley's note to a character in *Hellas* who suffers from

> that state of mind in which ideas may be supposed to assume the force of sensations through the confusion of thought with the objects of thought, and the excess of passion animating the creations of imagination. [Shelley, note to *Hellas*, l. 815; Bion, 1965, p. 133]

Shelley's Prometheus, "eyeless in hate", is the heroic victim of vengeful attacks of sensations (beta-elements) projected by a punitive superego, that make him unable to dream or form symbols. Bion would describe these as beta-elements resulting from attacks on linking; "Mental space is infinite"; so thought particles may be "dispersed instantaneously over infinite space" (Bion, 1970, p. 14). The remedy for Prometheus is that he has to learn a new language, through identification with a Muse-like figure (Asia), to "make strange combinations out of common things" (*Prometheus Unbound*, III.iii.: 32) and turn "crag-like agony" to "love" (IV: 560).

In Shelley's *The Triumph of Life*, an ambiguous female "Shape" comes to show the dreamer (Rousseau) "Whence I came, and where I am, and why", and the structure of his mind seems to disintegrate:

> As if the gazer's mind was strewn beneath
> Her feet like embers, and she, thought by thought,
> Trampled its sparks into the dust of death . . .
> [*The Triumph of Life*, ll. 386–388]

The shifting shapes of the Romantic psyche testify to their awareness that thoughts are separate from an apparatus for thinking; so there is a story to be told about the interaction between them. The Rousseau of Shelley's poem, desiring to re-dream his dream, in the midst of diffuse phantoms and shadows, is inspired by Dante to lead him on his quest: he who from hell

Love led serene, and who returned to tell
The words of hate and awe the wondrous story . . .

[ll. 474–475]

The way out of hell is through Love, Hate, and Awe, in partnership with an Other.

Bion saw Shelley in terms of having a "generous rivalry" with Keats, the last and most admired of the Romantic poets, eulogized in *Adonais*.[10] It was indeed Shelley's generosity that made him spokesman for all the poets, when he wrote:

Poets are the hierophants of an unapprehended inspiration, the mirrors of the gigantic shadows which futurity casts upon the present, the words which express what they understand not . . . Poets are the unacknowledged legislators of the world. [*Defence of Poetry*; 1977, p. 508]

Their metaphors presage ideas that only become explicit hundreds of years later. Bion is hinting at this famous passage when he talks of powerful ideas that are "buried in the future which has not happened" (1977, p. 43); and indeed Shelley's "shadow of futurity" lies behind, or rather in advance of, Bion's *Memoir of the Future*.

Shelley's generosity, a feature of a vision wider than the vehicle of its personality, contrasted—Bion thought—with the "envious rivalry" with Keats that emanated from Byron. Byron dismissed (his idea of) Keats with the lines:

'Tis strange the mind, that very fiery particle,
Should let itself be snuffed out by an article.

[*Don Juan*, XI: 60]

Nonetheless Byron, too, probably had some influence on Bion, particularly in relation to his existentialism (shared with Coleridge) and his efforts to make the extraordinary nature of Mind—that "fiery particle"—appear a real thing. Like Bion, he described its activities as "volcanic". "How can I explain that I can see intuitively that there is a Mind?" asks Bion (1973–1974, Vol. I, p. 60). How can he find the words to convey the reality of his question? "Immaterialism's a serious matter", punned Byron (*Don Juan*, XVI: 114). Dreams, he wrote in his journal, express the action of Mind and it is "much more Mind than when we are awake" (*Detached Thoughts* no. 96). Or, as he puts it satirically in *Don Juan*, with a Bionian turn of humour:

> "To be, or not to be?"—Ere I decide,
>     I should be glad to know that which *is being*.
> 'Tis true we speculate both far and wide,
>     And deem, because we *see*, we are *all-seeing*:
> For my part, I'll enlist on neither side,
>     Until I see both sides for once agreeing.
> For me, I sometimes think that Life is Death,
> Rather than Life a mere affair of breath. [*Don Juan*, IX: 16]

"I must rush", writes Bion, "I have a date to meet Fate" (1991, p. 577). The characters in the *Memoir* are always saying "of course" and being challenged for presumption by the others. Like Bion, Byron pre-empts the pre-empter ("Ere I decide"), the ignorant person who leaps into action without ever asking the question "what *is being?*" Yet at the same time, he was always leaping into action himself.[11] As he said, he empathized with both sides of an irreconcileable divide.

Byron felt himself in perpetual fight/flight mode, pursued by Woman or Poetry, a combined she-devil like some of Bion's nightmare female figures in the *Memoir* or *The Long Week-End*.[12] Byron lacked a Rosemary to keep these persecutors in order, and described his own mind as a "sad jar of atoms". He was fleeing, he was well aware, from the principle of Beauty itself, and the inherent ambiguities which less perceptive minds (the "all-seeing" sort) managed not to see. He longed for a "more Shakespearean" muse (Aurora in *Don Juan*) yet was not prepared to pay the price of emotional commitment; so it was ironic—and also understandable—that he could not tolerate the new Romantic baby-poet who was indeed more Shakespearean and more able to sustain aesthetic conflict.

The poems and letters of Keats embody a further quantum leap in the spiritual metaphysics that Milton set in motion; they encompass the probings and insights of the earlier Romantics and supersede them in the same way that his new goddess Psyche supersedes the "Old Olympians". No mental event is real, says Keats, until we "feel it on the pulses". He did not shirk the loneliness which Bion said could overwhelm the analyst who attains a necessary detach-ment from his primitive feelings and their somatic reality: on the contrary, he faced it squarely with "Heart, thou and I are here sad and alone", on the brink of his creative breakthrough of spring 1819. Like Blake and Keats, Bion often asks how we can recognize "the real thing" (in relation to love, for example (1991, p. 354), or indeed any authentic "conversation" (*ibid.*, p. 477). "I never feel certain of any truth but from a clear perception of its beauty", said Keats (letter to G. and G. Keats, December 1818–January 1819; 1970a, p. 187). Relatively late in his career Bion, too, admitted almost reluctantly that in his analytic practice he relied on an "aesthetic" sense to confirm the accuracy—that is, the reality—of an interpretation (1965, p. 38). "Could Beauty help?" asks his heroine Rosemary in the *Memoir*, in the context of trying to free "the fumbling infancy of psycho-analysis from the domain of sensuality-based mind" (1991, p. 130). Beauty, she suggests, has its own inher-ent abstracting quality comparable to mathematics.

Keats, along with some of the other Romantic poets, employed the new language of physics and chemistry to illuminate his concept of mental growth; and in a sense Bion, in his search of a language for non-sensuous phenomena, was drawing on the findings of twenti-eth-century science metaphorically rather than literally. Men of genius, said Keats, operate like "ethereal chemicals" on the "mass of intellect", a "spiritual yeast" arousing turbulence but also as-piration in the Group—a messianic idea without the manic aura. The poets used the term "particles" much as Bion used "elements", as when Keats described himself as "straining at particles of light in the midst of a great darkness" (letter to G. and G. Keats, February–May 1819; 1970a, p. 230). Keats's "particles" are in constant motion and, through "provings and alterings and perfectionings", refine their potential as "sparks of God's own essence" (alpha-elements). They are apparently random and infinite until attention catches them within the network of an individual mind, thoughts are elabo-rated, and an "identity" begins to form in a world that has become a "vale of Soulmaking". The "world of circumstances" is meaning-less except in relation to the eye of the beholder. Keats saw the mind–brain as a "tapestry empyrean" whose threads reached in all directions, much like Bion's notion of mental "polyvalency" (1997, p. 25).

Bion frequently used the "selected fact" of Poincaré and of Gestalt theory to describe the point at which meaningfulness enters in to the mind crowded with "particles" or "elements", such that the kaleidoscope is reconfigured and a pattern becomes visible in the chaos of chance (for example, 1977, p. 11). He also, however, had in mind Keats's early sonnet "On first looking into Chapman's Homer", in which the same type of illumination is described, more musically and memorably, and which begins:

> Then felt I like some watcher of the skies
> When a new planet swims into his ken . . .
> [cited in Bion, 1997, p. 29]

Or as Keats puts it in his "Ode to Psyche": "I see, and sing, by my own eyes inspired". In that seminal poem Keats, as one of Shelley's foreseeing "hierophants", attained the vision on which modern psychoanalysis is founded: the internal relationship between infant-poet and mother-muse as teaching object. Keats always focuses on the situation of the threshold between two key poles or internal figures, and establishes the tension between them in a way that delicately holds the psychic situation for observation, just as Bion always concentrates on the "caesura" or synapse and on linkages. In doing so, Keats pursued the implications of the other Romantic poets' phraseology to their logical conclusion: he was clear that—as Bion so often insisted—thoughts are not invented, but platonically pre-date their reception into earthly form. They enter into a mind that has developed an apparatus for thinking. This is the metaphorical "garden" of the "Ode to Psyche", where the poet–priest tends "the wreathed trellis of a working brain" and puts the mind in a condition of preparedness, ready to "let the warm Love in" and facilitate the creative conjunction of Cupid and Psyche.

It is moreover significant that Keats, like Milton, attained his orientation to "things invisible" after working his way out of the deep depression caused by the death of his beloved younger brother, Tom. Following this, Keats described his state of mind as one in which if he should fall into water he "would scarcely kick to come to the top". Tom was to John Keats as "Sweeting" was to Bion, Sweeting being the name he gave to the young runner during the war whose thoracic wall was blown off. Sweeting (whose actual name was Kitching) begged Bion to write to his mother, an emotional load which Bion felt to be intolerable. Near the end of his own life, Keats said his sister Fanny haunted him "like a ghost— she is so like Tom", and Bion, in his autobiographies, describes how he was forever haunted by the "ghosts" of his lost comrades. The young Bion and Keats were both in the situation of being mother to these even younger siblings.[13]

And from another perspective, they were both notably conscious of their debt to their creative predecessors ("ancestors", as Bion calls them), meaning all those who have contributed to their present mind or personality, including those in Bion's frequent refrain *"ante Agamemnona multi"* who may be unknown or unnamed. Bion's warnings about arrogance, and his description of his "inchoate ambitions" and sense of unworthiness at school, are prefigured in the teenage Keats's question: "Who am I to be a poet, seeing how great a thing it is?" (letter to Hunt, 10 May 1817; 1970a, p. 10). Indeed, Keats's search for "the true voice of feeling" and his recognition of the difficulty of finding it,[14] could summarize for Bion the heart of his own struggle over many decades: how to convey the fact that he *meant it*.

Keats's model of the mind was earned through "suffering" in the Bionian sense of "neither fighting nor running away" (Bion, 1961, p. 65). "Until we are sick, we understand not" (Keats, letter to Reynolds, 3 May 1818; 1970a, p. 93). Much could be said about Keats's later satire about anti-poetry in *Lamia*, with its persecutory "buzzing thoughts" in the spirit of the Negative Grid, and about "sad Moneta", the frozen Muse of *The Fall of Hyperion* and the possible influence on Bion's portrayal of the war-struck mother. To conclude this brief account, however, we can simply highlight the deep impression that Keats's doctrine of "Negative Capability" made on Bion. Keats formulated it early in his career, but came to live it out in his subsequent great poetry and in his life, and this is what gave it weight and substance for Bion, as indeed for all of us. It became the phrase that Bion felt expressed better than he could himself the need to tolerate the frustration of not-knowing. The use of "negative" here is, of course, different from Blake's, or the Negative Grid: it locates the space between impulse and action in which the mind makes itself available for thinking, allowing sufficient time—even one pulsation of an artery—for the thoughts to germinate. Unless strength is developed in this area, all attempts at conducting a psychoanalysis are futile. Keats was—as Shelley divined—the stain on the radiance of eternity (the blush on the walls of the uterus) that embodied the "growing germ of thought" for psychoanalytic thinkers in the shadow of futurity. It is fitting that Keats's epitaph at Rome—"here lies one whose name was writ in water"—comes to Bion's mind to describe the ephemeral nature of the psychoanalytic conversation itself:

> It is difficult because the conversation is really as it were written in water. The water closes in immediately on top of it. So it does depend on having some system of recording it, mentally. [Bion, Tavistock talk of 1977, cited from tape transcript]

It is, as Keats himself said, a "ditty of no tone".


## Notes

1. Elsewhere, of course, Bion notes the further possibility that genuine ideas may vanish when their host is "loaded with honours and sunk without trace" (1970, p. 78).
2. Bion cites the Latin original in his seminar given in 1977 in Rome; the editor gives the reference as Horace, *Odes*, IV: 9.
3. The anthology was never completed or published; Francesca Bion quotes this extract in her "Envoi" to *All My Sins Remembered*.
4. See Milton's preface to *The Reason of Church Government Urged against Prelaty* (1642; 2003, p. 640), where he distinguishes the Platonic idea of the good from its cultural mask, "custom and awe".
5. The name Bedlam derives from that of an early English mental asylum (originally "Bethlehem").
6. Both Bion and Milton had wives who died in childbirth—Milton shortly before beginning *Paradise Lost*, when he was also newly blind. He never saw his wife's face.
7. The beta-screen displays an unconscious agglomeration of "beta-elements", which cannot be used in thinking, though they may be used for hallucination, since they are either expelled mental residue or untransformed (meaningless) sense-impressions.
8. See for example Blake, *Jerusalem*, plate 3; Bion, 1965, p. 38; Milton, *Paradise Lost*, VII: 126.

9. Cited, though not attributed, in Bion, 1970, p. 46.

10. Bion recorded his views after visiting the Keats–Shelley memorial in Rome (Bion, 1992, p. 369). Byron satirised Keats in *Don Juan* as having been a non-serious poet who was "killed off by a critique" (*Don Juan* XI, 1. 60). Byron and Shelley between them initiated a wrong-headed myth about Keats which endured until modern times. *Adonais* was probably more Shelley's elegy for his own son, who had recently died, than for this sibling poet.

11. Byron died in search of "a soldier's grave" after joining the Greek fight for independence ("On this day I complete my thirty-sixth year").

12. For example the "nurse" who appears to project a lethal dose of shell-shock into a wounded soldier (Bion, 1982, p. 193); or the Old Woman who terrifies him (p. 145).

13. I speculate that my father, Roland Harris, was another of those siblings, whom Bion might possibly have felt he abandoned in mid-analysis when he left London for California, in his urgency to escape from the tank of the British Psychoanalytic Society. My father died suddenly and unexpectedly the year after Bion left. Bion has said that he owed his own "continued existence to [his] capacity to fear 'an impending disaster'" (1991, p. 175).

14. Keats, letter to Reynolds, 21 September 1819; 1970a, p. 292.

# REFERENCES

Bion, W. R. (1961). *Experiences in Groups*. London: Heinemann.

Bion, W. R. (1963). *Elements of Psychoanalysis*. London: Heinemann.

Bion, W. R. (1965). *Transformations*. London: Heinemann.

Bion, W. R. (1967). *Second Thoughts*. London: Heinemann.

Bion, W. R. (1970). *Attention and Interpretation*. London: Tavistock.

Bion, W. R. (1973–1974). *Brazilian Lectures* (2 vols). Rio de Janeiro: Imago.

Bion, W. R. (1977). *Two Papers: The Grid and Caesura*, J. Salomao (Ed.). São Paulo: Imago.

Bion, W. R. (1982). *The Long Week-End*. Abingdon: Fleetwood Press.

Bion, W. R. (1985). *All My Sins Remembered*, F. Bion (Ed.). Abingdon: Fleetwood Press.

Bion, W. R. (1991). *A Memoir of the Future* (3 Vols. 1975, 1977, 1979). London: Karnac.

Bion, W. R. (1992). *Cogitations*, F. Bion (Ed.). London: Karnac.

Bion, W. R. (1997). *Taming Wild Thoughts*, F. Bion (Ed.). London: Karnac.

Bion, W. R. (2005a). *Italian Seminars*, P. Slotkin (Trans.). London: Karnac.

Bion, W. R. (2005b). *The Tavistock Seminars*. London: Karnac.

Blake, W. (1966). *Complete Writings*, G. Keynes (Ed.). Oxford: Oxford University Press.

Coleridge, S. T. (1957). *Notebooks*, K. Coburn (Ed.), 3 vols. London: Routledge.

Coleridge, S. T. (1960). *Shakespeare Criticism*, T. M. Raysor (Ed.), 2 vols. London: Dent.

Coleridge, S. T. (1969). *Poetical Works*. London: Oxford University Press.

Coleridge, S. T. (1972). The Statesman's Manual (1816). In: R. J. White (Ed.), *Lay Sermons* (pp. 1–280). London: Routledge.

Corbett, J. (1944). *Man-Eaters of Kumaon*. Reprinted Delhi: Oxford University Press, 1988.

Eliot, T. S. (1944). *Four Quartets*. London: Faber.

Golding, W. (1956). *Pincher Martin*. Reprinted Faber, 2005.

Harris, M. (1987a). Bion's conception of a psycho-analytical attitude (1980). In: M. H. Williams (Ed.), *Collected Papers of Martha Harris and Esther Bick* (pp. 340–344). Strathtay, Perthshire: Clunie Press.

Harris, M. (1987b). The individual in the group: on learning to work with the psychoanalytical method (1978). In: M. H. Williams (Ed.) *Collected Papers of Martha Harris and Esther Bick* (pp. 322–339). Strathtay, Perthshire: Clunie Press.

Harris, R. J. (*ca* 1938–1950). *Poems*, unpublished.

Harris, R. J. (1970). *Poems*. Strath Tay, Perthshire: Clunie Press.

Hopkins, G. M. (1953). *The Hopkins Reader*, J. Pick (Ed.). London: Oxford University Press.

Keats, J. (1970a). *Selected Letters*, R. Gittings (Ed.). Oxford: Oxford University Press.

Keats, J. (1970b). *Poems*, M. Allott (Ed.). London: Longman.

Marvell, A. (1952). *Poems* (1681), H. MacDonald (Ed.). London: Routledge.

Mawson, C. (Ed.) (2010). *Bion Today*. London: Routledge.

Meltzer, D. (1983). *Dream Life*. Strathtay, Perthshire: Clunie Press.

Meltzer, D. (1992). *The Claustrum*. Strathtay, Perthshire: Clunie Press [reprinted London: Karnac, 2008].

Meltzer, D., & Williams, M. H. (1988). *The Apprehension of Beauty*. Strathtay, Perthshire: Clunie Press [reprinted London: Karnac, 2008].

Milton, J. (1972). Letter to a Friend. In: *Trinity College Manuscript* (facsimile edition) (pp. 6–7), W. A. Wright, (Ed.). Menston: Scolar Press.

Milton, J. (2003). *Complete Poems and Major Prose*, M. Y. Hughes (Ed.). Indianapolis, IN: Hackett.

Olney, J. (1980). Autobiography and the cultural moment. In: *Autobiography: Essays Theoretical and Critical* (pp. 3–27). Princeton, NJ: Princeton University Press.

Owen, W. (1990). *Poems* (1920), J. Stallworthy (Ed.). London: Chatto & Windus.

Plato (1975). *Phaedrus*, W. Hamilton (Trans.). Harmondsworth: Penguin.

Plato (1987). *Theaetetus*, R. Waterfield (Trans.). Harmondsworth: Penguin.

Shelley, P. B. (1977). *Poetry and Prose*, D. H. Reiman & S. B. Powers (Eds.). New York: Norton.

Trotter, W. (1916). *Instincts of the Herd in Peace and War*. Reprinted New York: Cosimo Classics, 2005.

Williams, M. H. (1983a). "Underlying pattern" in Bion's *Memoir of the Future*. *International Review of Psycho-Analysis*, *10*(75): 75–86 [reprinted in C. Mawson (Ed.), *Bion Today*, Routledge, 2010].

Williams, M. H. (1983b). Bion's *The Long Week-End*: a review article. *Journal of Child Psychotherapy*, *9*: 69–79.

Williams, M. H. (1985). The Tiger and "O". *Free Associations*, *1*: 33–55.

Williams, M. H. (2005a). Confessions of an emmature superego, or, the ayah's lament. In: *The Vale of Soulmaking: the post-Kleinian model of the mind and its poetic origins* (pp. 221–240). London: Karnac.

Williams, M. H. (2005b). Rosemary's roots: the Muse in Bion's autobiographies. In: *The Vale of Soulmaking: the post-Kleinian model of the mind and its poetic origins* (pp. 201–220). London: Karnac.

Williams, M. H. (2009). As musas do psicanalista. In: *Colecao Memoria da psicanalise*, Vol. 6, pp. 90–97, G. Costa Pinto (Ed.). Sao Paulo: Duetto.

Williams, M. H. (2010). *The Aesthetic Development: The Poetic Spirit of Psychoanalysis*. London: Karnac.

Made in the USA
Middletown, DE
11 August 2023

36581612R00066